A Funny Thing Happened On The Way To The Honeymooners...

I Had A Life

A Funny Thing Happened On The Way To The Honeymooners...
I Had A Life

by Jane Kean
as told to
Kris Paradis

BearManor Media
2003

A Funny Thing Happened on the Way to the Honeymooners…I Had a Life
© 2003 by Jane Kean. All rights reserved.

Published in the USA by

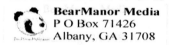

BearManor Media
P O Box 71426
Albany, GA 31708

bearmanormedia.com

Cover design by John Teehan
Typesetting and layout by John Teehan

ISBN—0-97174570-9-3

Table of Contents

Preface

The last *Honeymooners* Special was broadcast from the stage of the Resorts International Hotel in Atlantic City in 1978. As Audrey Meadows and I walked through the lobby one day, two very excited middle-aged ladies spotted us and remarked, "Oh! There goes What's-her-name, and there's the other one!"

Since I'm not sure if I was "What's-her-name" or "the other one," I feel I need to clarify my identity and let you know who I was before Trixie...

I Just Wanted The Bike

I was born in my home in Hartford, Connecticut, where my father, Robert Kean, worked for an insurance company. My older sister, Betty, was a natural born performer and my mother, Helen, encouraged her interest in show business from an early age. Helen was fascinated by the entertainment business and made sure Betty had great training.

Betty went to the same dancing school that Eleanor Powell attended, The Ralph McKernan Dancing School in Springfield, Massachusetts. McKernan was the first teacher to combine ballet with tap. My father refused to pay for dancing lessons so my mother played the piano at the school to pay for the lessons.

I never had lessons. I was always a faker.

When I was four, I was encouraged to make my first stage appearance. Mother promised me a bicycle if I would sing "Telling It to the Daisies." I had a little routine where I did a heel stretch and a cartwheel. My mother was convinced it was remarkable. I just wanted the bike.

I walked out on stage and, holy cow, my first case of stage fright. I just choked. I turned to my mother backstage and said, "I'm just not gonna do it," and walked right off. Betty rushed in with a tap dance, pirouettes and a walkover. Family honor was saved but I wanted to die right there on the stage of the Bushnell Memorial Theater.

By the time she was fifteen, Betty had her own radio show in Hartford with a fellow who played the piano and sang. The show was called *Betty and Burt*. I remember the opening… "Are you havin' any fun? Are you doin' any livin'? What good is what you've got, if you're not havin' any fun…"

Betty was eight years older than I and was already having quite a bit of fun with a visiting star baseball player by the name of Van "Lingo" Mungo.

Hartford may have been a booming insurance town but it was definitely not the place to be if you wanted to make it in show business. Mother concluded we needed to be in New York but my father firmly opposed the idea. After a lot of arguing, time, and energy, Mother won out.

My father's six sisters had always been convinced that Mother was not good enough for their brother. This new turn sealed the deal. They never spoke to my mother again.

My father was let go by the insurance company in Hartford. That was the only time we really had no money. I was eight years old and, like Scarlett, I swore I would never be hungry again.

We drove to New York in Daddy's Hup Mobile and ate at the AutoMat. You could put a nickel in a slot and get the best sweet roll and hot chocolate you ever tasted. A twelve-course meal cost about two dollars. While we were there, I looked down on the floor and found a twenty-dollar bill. It was like finding two hundred today. That kept us eating for a week.

Betty, Mother and I checked into one room in the President Hotel on West 48th Street. It wasn't much but my mother had a gift of turning any place we lived into something cozy and livable.

In 1933 Betty got a job in the Vaudeville show following the film *The Gold Diggers* at the Earl Theater in Philadelphia. Robert Alton was the choreographer. He had studied at the same school in Springfield so he knew Betty. He made her one of the "Gold Digger" ensemble. During the show, Betty caught her heel in the stage's turntable, took the whole line down with her and was fired.

Bob wanted to help Betty out so he gave her a job on the truck that went through town advertising the show. The girls on the truck were dressed in "Gold Digger" costumes and threw gold coins to people on the street. My father, mother and I were in the Hup Mobile right behind the truck to make sure nothing happened to her. She was only fifteen.

Daddy went to Syracuse and took a job with the Traveler's Insurance Company. Mother was not about to go live in Syracuse. It was not her style. So, Daddy came down to see us every two or three weeks. After about a year, Mother felt obliged to visit him, so she and I drove to Syracuse. When he opened the door, a woman came out of the bedroom in her underwear. My mother grabbed my hand and we left. We never went back there again.

I attended public school while Betty auditioned for shows. She quickly got an agent who placed her in *George White's Music Hall Varieties* starring Harry Richman, Bert Lahr and Eleanor Powell. Betty was put in sketches with Bert Lahr but was not allowed to dance since she had the same dancing style as Eleanor. That was probably the beginning of her comedic development. She was very funny.

Mother didn't think Betty was very funny when she eloped at seventeen.

We went up to the theater where Betty was playing but she wasn't there. When we asked around, the other acts were all hushed up. Betty had run off between acts with this much older comedian, Roy Sedley, who was about thirty-four. Very funny guy but not my mother's choice.

Roy drank heavily and had been known to drop his pants on stage. He evidently was dropping them offstage as well because Betty became pregnant almost immediately. When Mother discovered this, she stood on the radiator of our 12th floor apartment with the window open. She took me by the hand and screamed, "Come on, Jane, I can't take it anymore!"

I was crying and screaming, "I don't want to go...*you* go!"

Betty pulled from the inside, promising to get an abortion and an annulment. Mother finally stepped down but I do believe she would have done it.

After Betty got an annulment, she went on the road with a Vaudeville act. Mother and I stayed in New York because I was still in school. When Betty got a dancing gig at the famed Trocadero in Hollywood around 1938-39, Mother and I joined her there. Betty stopped the show cold. She was such a hit that night, they asked her to return the following Sunday. Betty met Jack Benny after the show. He recognized her gift for comedy and suggested she work more of it into her act.

Mother told Betty to use me in the show the following week. All I could do was the Jitterbug and a little song. I had done it in Philadelphia once before and it had been a big hit. We bought matching dresses at Nancy's on Hollywood Boulevard and prepared for our routine.

Sunday night arrived. It was a truly star-studded evening. Sonja Henie and Tyrone Power, Carole Lombard and Clark Gable were in the audience. Betty did her number first then brought me on and we did a Jitterbug together. We laid such an egg and were so embarrassed that we hid in the ladies room with our feet up on the toilet so no one would recognize our shoes. We waited until everyone had left.

Yet another setback for my career. It was evident that I needed more experience.

Betty, Jane and Helen

Helen and Robert Kean

Older sister Betty with Jane

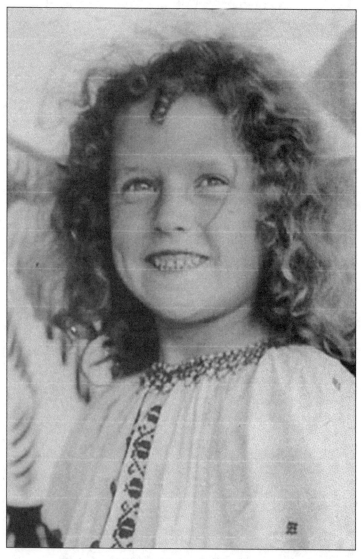

Mother was convinced I was the next Shirley Temple

Mickey

In spite of my inexperience, an agent from William Morris thought I was a natural for the Andy Hardy movies. I was fifteen and had a voice that could be heard in Pasadena. My audition for producer Lew Ostrow at MGM was a big success. I was to test with Mickey Rooney, so Harry Friedman from the WM office took me over to the set to meet him.

Mickey got my phone number from Harry and called me that night for a date. What a thrill! Every teenager in America had a crush on him and I was no exception. And smooth! Oh, my Lord. I could see why Ava Gardner and all those beauties he married fell in love with him. What a line he had!

I was inexperienced in affairs of the heart and was devastated when, after several dates Mickey's friend, Sidney Miller, called to cancel our next date. Mickey had to work late, Sidney said, so we wouldn't be going to the fights with his mom. He would have called me himself but he was tied up.

That was the end of it. There was no test at MGM and no more word from the popular young star.

Years later, I was on Broadway in *Will Success Spoil Rock Hunter?* Mickey called to invite me to the track and out to dinner. We always had fun with a little romance thrown in. He was a great kisser.

We eventually appeared together in several productions including *No Sex Please* at the Coconut Grove in Florida and the old reliable, *Three Goats in a Blanket. Three Goats* was a perfect venue for him and he did it so much, he started changing the name so bookers would think they were getting a new show. He called it "Alimony," and "The Laugh's on Me," but it was still just *Three Goats.* I loved playing his ex-wife and sometimes we'd ad-lib a whole scene.

A lot of actors didn't enjoy working with him because of his ad-libbing, but it never bothered me. I actually loved it. After all, he was Mickey Rooney! He'd been a star since he was four years old. He was a truly great performer and could do virtually anything.

When we were appearing in Miami, he handed out bumper stickers that said, "Honk! If you've been married to Mickey Rooney!" I got a lot of honks with mine.

With Mickey Rooney and Sammy Davis, Jr. at the Harwyn in New York

You Must Want My Sister!

My mother was a control freak. She could control me but never Betty. Betty loved to have a good time. She loved to drink and smoke. She also loved my mother but Betty was a free spirit.

Mother said to me, "If you smoke and drink, you'll break my heart."

I didn't want to break her heart, so I never did.

Betty was married five times in all and always used to say, "My sister is the pretty one, but I'm the live one!"

One morning, I was awakened at 7 o'clock by the ringing phone. I answered and the voice on the other end said, "Is this Jane Kean?"

"Yes," I replied sleepily.

The man on the other end of the phone said, "Well, I'd like to f— you."

"Oh," I said. "You must want my sister."

I went in the other room and woke her up.

"It's for you," I said.

She got on the phone.

"Who's this?" asked the voice.

"This is Betty," she replied.

"Well, I'd like to f— you, too!"

Betty hung up, furious. "Why'd you do that?"

"I don't know," I said. "You've been married twice. I thought it had to be for you."

Because Betty was the way she was, Mother was overly protective of me. She watched me like a hawk. No man was ever good enough. If I was close to someone, she'd say, So-and-so's an awfully nice guy, but he's kind of square, don't you think? Just a little square for you?

That made me think, Oh…yeah! He *is* square! Then it was a big turnoff.

She never said, "Don't marry him." Nothing so direct. She knew just how to handle me. She wanted to keep me with her and it worked. I stayed with my mother until the day she died. I was thirty-four when she passed away and I was married within the year.

Sometime later, when I returned to Hollywood with my mother, we were once again in pursuit of Betty who was having an affair with a wild comedian who was known as Lord Buckley. He couldn't have been farther from royalty.

Lord Buckley was appearing at The It Café at the Hollywood Plaza on Vine Street. Mother and I had a room there. One night, the Lord set his room on fire while smoking pot and burned us all out. My dad cashed in an insurance policy and bailed us out of the hotel so we could rent an apartment on Formosa Avenue.

Betty went back to New York to work for Nils Thor Grantlund at the Swedish-themed Midnight Sun. Granny, as NTG was called, was behind in salaries and Betty was being paid off in smorgasbord. Since Betty couldn't help us out with the rent, my dad came through again.

When I started out, they didn't have all the heavy microphones the way they do today. I studied voice with Al Siegel who had been Ethel Merman's coach. Al would make me scream "HELP!" at the top of my lungs. I got so loud that we had people beating on the studio door trying to save me.

Al helped me put together a few songs that I could use as an act. Leo Cohen, the booker for the Loew's Theaters, put me on the bill at Loew's State with Ed Sullivan and the Harvest Moon Dancers. Every year, Sullivan would take the winners of the Harvest Moon Contest and act as M.C. for them at the theater on Broadway. After the State engagement, the show toured all the Loew's Theaters in the five boroughs surrounding the city.

I was one of the four other acts on the bill. I had the number two spot; three songs, exit and one encore. I didn't have any special material or fabulous arrangements. We didn't need them then. A chorus and a half in the key of G with a big ending. That was it.

I had just turned eighteen and this seemed like a big break for me. Being on the bill with Sullivan usually generated publicity, especially in his column in *The Daily News*.

I was extremely flattered every time he stood in the wings and watched my act. Mother had seen to it that I had a fabulous wardrobe. Lots of beads and cleavage.

At the end of the State engagement, Sullivan requested that I play the other theaters with him. Wow! I was on cloud nine.

Most of them were anywhere from forty-five minutes to an hour away. Sullivan was nice enough to offer me a ride to and from the theaters. At the end of every ride home, he would get affectionate, starting with a kiss on the cheek. Eventually, he got a little more aggressive and suggested I fondle him in a certain area which shall remain nameless. I declined.

After one show, he invited me to his personal suite at the Delmonico Hotel on Park Avenue. I declined again.

The closing night of the tour, he suggested I invite him up for a cup of coffee to celebrate the end of the tour. I didn't think that would be bad because my mother was usually there.

When we entered the apartment, I found Helen had gone out to dinner and the theater. Sullivan wasted no time. He pushed me down on the couch and got on top of me. He exposed himself and ripped off my underwear. I tried to fight him off but he was strong as an ox. He had been a fighter in his youth and he definitely won this round.

I was terrified and ashamed. He kissed me on the cheek and said "goodnight."

For the next two weeks, I walked around in a fog. I kept running to the bathroom to see if I had my period. Mother questioned me about my strange behavior and I finally had to tell the truth. She immediately called Ed and asked him over to our apartment for a meeting. I was mortified.

She asked him all the lurid details. Did he penetrate completely? Did he withdraw at the right time?

He assured her he had taken the necessary precautions and that there was nothing to worry about. That didn't satisfy me. I continued to worry until I got my period.

I finally said to Helen, "Don't you think it's about time you told me more about the birds and the bees?"

I don't think she knew that much. She was married at seventeen. Two kids, boom, boom, and that was it. She was only thirty-five when she moved to New York. She was a handsome woman but she never had a boyfriend. I'm convinced she didn't care much about sex or men.

Sullivan continued to call me and he sent me love notes when he went to Florida. He claimed he was in love with me and would send messages through Carmine, his assistant who was also backstage manager at Loew's Theater.

Ed never had the reputation of being a ladies man or a player but he was. Unaccustomed to so much attention, I was becoming more and more attracted to him. In my eighteen-year-old eyes, he began to resemble Humphrey Bogart. *Casablanca* was my favorite movie.

Sullivan paid me $25 to appear on his second television show called *Toast of the Town* featuring the June Taylor dancers. *Variety* said I was one of the few women that televised successfully. The bad lighting was very unflattering to most women. Everyone in the early shows wore black lipstick and heavy pancake makeup. Looking good was a major challenge.

Ed's show was a big success. It was one of the early hits that sustained popularity for many years due to his ability to attract the hottest acts. As he became more involved with his show, his interest in me waned somewhat. I still continued to hear from him, but we were both busy, busy, busy.

With Jackie Coogan at Loew's State, 1945.

A Real Belter

My first Broadway show was a musical called *Early to Bed*. Fats Waller wrote the music. When the reviews came out, they said I was the "likely successor to Ethel Merman." You could hear me all over the theater. I was a real belter. It was the yelling "Help" that did it.

Kay Thompson was a belter, too. She was also a great arranger. Before she created "Eloise," she was on Perry Como's show, among others. She enjoyed great success in her act with the Williams Brothers and later in the movie, *Funny Face* with Audrey Hepburn. Kay took me on as a protégé when I was about eighteen and gave me a lot of her arrangements. She was a wonderful accompanist and played at my audition for *Early to Bed*. I'm convinced that helped me get the show. She sounded like a whole band. Kay was later Liza Minnelli's godmother after working with Judy Garland at MGM.

Early to Bed gave me my first exposure to professional jealousy. Mary Small used to trip me as I went on stage for my bow. She was miffed because I got a song she wanted. We had one number together called "The Ladies Who Sing with the Band." She sometimes pinched me in the back during the number. The stagehands would say, "We see what she's doin' to ya. Why don't ya say somethin'!" When I complained to producer and leading man, Dick Kollmar, he just stared. That's showbiz.

Charles Feldman saw me in *Early to Bed* in 1943. Feldman and Blum were one of the biggest talent agencies in Hollywood at the time. Feldman offered me $200 a week for six weeks plus fare for my Mother's and me to Hollywood. He guaranteed me a contract after the six weeks. He got me a test with the top cameraman at 20th Century-Fox and they signed me. Fox already had two-dozen perky blondes who were already established. So, I just sat there and collected a good salary for six months.

My mother and I went away one weekend and I got a call from Zanuck's office.

"How dare you go away without telling us. You were supposed to make a test with William Bendix. You can't just leave town without getting permission. We own you!"

A love scene with William Bendix? All I could think was: Why couldn't it be Tyrone Power?

Betty had an old jalopy parked in front of our apartment. I didn't really know how to drive but our apartment was very close to Fox, so, I cautiously drove to the studio. When I finished there, I backed that jalopy right into Darryl Zanuck's car. No wonder I never made a movie there.

After my option was up, I was finally offered a part in a movie but Mother wanted to return to New York to see what Betty was doing. So away we went, once more in pursuit of Betty.

The day before we arrived, Betty had eloped with Jim Backus, otherwise known as "Mr. Magoo." I guess she didn't want to risk Mother's interference. I really liked Jimmy a lot. He was the nicest husband she had ever brought home.

Unfortunately the marriage was of short duration. Betty went to San Francisco to do the *Ziegfeld Follies* and fell in love with the director. Poor Jimmy. It hit him so hard. He carried a torch for her for a long time after that.

Once we got settled back in New York, I got the lead in *The Girl from Nantucket*. When my father saw the marquee for this, my first starring role, he could only say, "Isn't that an awful lot of responsibility? What if it flops?" Talk about the kiss of death. Try as I may, I'll never forget those reviews. Here's my favorite:

> "'The Girl from Nantucket!' Duck it!"
> — *The World Telegram*

At least I didn't get slammed personally and that, of course, pleased Mother.

> "The turkey arrived a week before Thanksgiving...
> (Jane Kean) a bright blonde sight for sore eyes amongst
> the rotten eggs of the evening."
> —*The World Tribune*

Nantucket ran about six weeks. Six weeks of pure hell. The producer, Bob Ritchie, was a playboy with little knowledge of theater. His interests lay in the general direction of the gorgeous showgirls and the specific direction of a leggy redhead named Temple Texas. Va-va-va-voom.

This debacle was not the end of my career, however. I was signed to do *Are You With It?* on Broadway. Lew Parker was in the cast but I seldom saw him. When he was not on stage he was holed up in his dressing room reading the racing form. Years later, Lew would become Betty's fifth husband.

When Bob Hope went to Hollywood in the thirties to pursue his movie career, he sold Lew his vaudeville act for which Lew promised to pay him later. Whenever I would run into Bob anywhere, he would always yell, "Will you tell your brother-in-law to pay me for my act?" He only wanted what was coming to him. Lew probably bet it on a horse.

Jane Deering and Jane Kean in Early to Bed

With Jack Durant in The Girl from Nantucket...*Duck it!*

1947 cheesecake

Theatre-By-The-Sea

In 1951 Betty and I agreed to appear in Matunuck, Rhode Island for the whole summer season. The Theatre-By-The-Sea was located about 100 feet from the beach. We had the idea to call our friend Jackie Gleason and suggest that he bring his family up there for a month. We had recently appeared together on Broadway in *Along Fifth Avenue*.

Management was only willing to offer him $250 a week but they would provide the Gleasons with two suites and dining room privileges. Jackie agreed provided they'd have a bottle of scotch at his table each night. He also could choose any vehicle he wanted and they'd stage it. He chose *The Show Off*, a part he'd always wanted to play.

Jackie had recently reunited with his first wife, Genevieve, on the advice of Fulton Sheen, who was a close friend and Archbishop of the Catholic Church. Jackie was a Catholic and Genevieve was devout. They had two daughters, ages eleven and thirteen.

The theater was a typical, summer barn/theater with the usual live things flying around. One night we were in the middle of a very dramatic scene when a spider came down from the ceiling and hung right between the two of us. Jackie stopped the dialogue, and squished it using the old line, "That's the last show you'll see for nothing!"

An old joke but we laughed until we cried. They had to ring down the curtain. We couldn't get the script back on track.

Jackie was a big hit in *The Show Off* and stayed on to direct *Pal Joey*, which was also a smash. We were joined throughout the summer with appearances by Butterfly McQueen, Lionel Stander, Signe Hasso, and Sylvia Sidney.

Also in the company was Helmut Dantine, who was often cast as a Nazi in World War II movies. One night while I was babysitting my two-year-old niece, Helmut came down the fire escape and entered my room. He was a wild man, with eyes like Ralph Fiennes. One of his favorite tricks was to grab me in the wings on my exit and then send me back on stage with lipstick smeared all over my face. One such scene was with actress Edith Atwater. I don't think she was amused. And neither was my fiancé, Abbott Van Nostrand, who was the head of Samuel French Play Publishers. He thought our love scenes were too realistic and broke off the engagement.

I was obviously not ready for marriage yet. Abbott deserved someone who was willing to give everything up, settle down and take care of his three small children. His first wife had died at the age of thirty. He was listed on the Social Register, was quite handsome and very much in demand. He had no trouble finding a mate.

There was no place to go in Matunuck after the show so we set up a little stage in the dining room. Many of us who were appearing in the theater would strut our stuff in a kind of informal cabaret.

Jackie and I worked out a few bits together and tried them out there. He wrote a ditty for us that went, "I'm Jackie. I'm Janie. We're really very zany." He did his impression of Peter Lorre to my Bette Davis and we just kept playing off one another. The audiences roared.

Soon after, Jackie got *The Life of Riley* on television. He called me from California and suggested I fly out and meet with some writers who would write us an act for Las Vegas. He preferred to do sketches rather than stand-up. That wasn't his forte. I was really tempted but Betty and I were just beginning to work together. My mother wanted to keep it that way. So I had to decline.

Years later, when Jackie was number one at CBS, I ran into him. He reminded me of that decision and said, "Well, pal, you could have been there with me!" It would have been nice but I would have missed a lot of good things that happened to me on the way.

The rest of the summer was great fun. Betty and I both got the plays we wanted to do. I chose *Born Yesterday* with Lionel Stander and Betty chose Stander to have an affair with. Mother was about to have a fit over Betty's affair with Stander. I'm just glad it wasn't me.

Ed Sullivan made a surprise visit to see one of the shows and his favorite leading lady. Everyone was overwhelmed by his presence. I must admit, I was more surprised than anyone that he'd make the trip to Matunuck. Maybe it was love.

Butterfly McQueen will never be forgotten for her part in *Gone with the Wind*. She was a riot in the role of a maid in *No Time for Comedy* that summer. At one point in the play, Butterfly had to answer the phone and say where one of the characters was but she was forever forgetting her lines. She would say, "Just a minute, please..." into the phone, then run off to her dressing room to look at the script, and back on to the stage to resume. After the show, she dressed in island costume and sang Calypso in the cabaret. Vince Edwards, a winner of the Mr. Universe contest, was also there for the season playing small parts in several different productions. The parts grew smaller after they saw what a terrible actor he was. In spite of his lack of talent on the stage, he had plenty in the looks department and I thoroughly enjoyed watching him pump iron. He later became a hit with his television series *Ben Casey*. Women all over the U.S. were offering to play doctor with him.

One of the staff actors that summer was Ray Arnett, who later became Liberace's producer and choreographer for 26 years. He used to perform in the club, too.

Linda and Geraldine Gleason

I Love Lucy, Too!

Tom Rogers was a dear friend who worked in public relations at the MGM office in New York. He came to see my 1945 show, *Are You With It?*, and brought the young movie actress, Lucille Ball. After the show, he brought Lucy backstage. She invited me to lunch the next day and we really hit it off. We shopped all afternoon and went to see Desi at the Copacabana that night. He was great and the audience went wild when he introduced Lucy.

Lucy and I started spending a lot of time together. We went to shows and shopped to kill time until Desi finished up at the Copa. Sometimes, we would hang out in the Copa lounge until he was through. Nat King Cole and his trio were also playing there.

One of Lucy's early movies was playing in a theater on 42nd Street. She wanted me to see it, so we strutted over there and sat upstairs in the balcony. We had to leave the show early because we began to itch. The theater had fleas! Good thing they cleaned up that area.

After she went back to the coast, we continued to keep in touch. She would call whenever she was coming to New York and asked me to keep my time open for her while she was in town.

On one visit, she checked into the Hampshire House. Her room was decorated with pictures of birds and she asked the manager to remove them. She was very superstitious about airborne creatures. It's a good thing Hitchcock didn't offer her the lead in *The Birds*.

While Desi was still at the Copa, he called in sick and the three of us went to Saratoga to the races. Desi loved the horses. I had never been to the track and was making two-dollar bets on the horses with names I liked. I was the only winner that day and Desi lost about three thousand dollars. That's beginner's luck for you. Someone there saw Desi and told Jack Entratter at the Copa. Apparently, Desi caught a little hell.

Another first for me was when they took me to Miami where Desi was working at the Brook Club. I'd never been to Florida before and it was quite a kick. Desi took us fishing one morning at 5 a.m. When we returned, Desi cleaned our fish and cooked them. Delicious!

The Brook Club had a casino and Desi dropped a bundle there opening night. Lucy had a fit.

She had another fit when Mother followed me to Florida. Upon her arrival, Mother insisted that I stay with her at her hotel, so that was the end of the adventure. Lucy and Desi were not about to hang out with my mom.

However, when we all went back to New York, Helen cooked a wonderful dinner for them. Whenever we had guests, she was the life of the party. She got everyone around the piano when she played, "Let Me Call You Sweetheart."

It will probably come as no surprise that one of my best roles was later in *Gypsy*. I played Mama Rose for three months at the Beverly Dinner Theater in New Orleans. Not much research needed for that role. I had been living with Mama Rose for years!

Although Lucy didn't dislike Helen, she felt strongly that I needed to let go of the apron strings and live on my own. She was probably right, but it was difficult to break that bond. I enjoyed my mother's company so much.

Are You With It? *with Johnny Downs and Lew Parker*

At home with Lucy and Desi in Chatsworth, B.B.H. (Before Beverly Hills)

Lucy and Jane in Las Vegas

Jane and Dede Ball (Lucy's mom) in 1967 in Stockbridge, Massachusetts

Frank Fay

Frank Fay had been a giant star in Vaudeville and created the character Elwood P. Dowd in *Harvey* on Broadway. With those almost translucent blue eyes, he made you believe he actually saw that rabbit. Frank established the precedent of doing a curtain speech after the play. He would come out and just talk to the audience. He and the director argued about it but Frank insisted and won out. After he left the show, everyone who succeeded him did an after-curtain speech. I personally thought it was wrong that they didn't give him the part in the film version of *Harvey*. Even though Jimmy Stewart did a good job, no one could top Frank in that role. And I am not personally partial to Frank Fay.

Frank was married to Barbara Stanwyck in the Catholic Church in 1928. They adopted a child and lived in a beautiful home in Brentwood. Barbara left him in the middle of the night and didn't take one thing. She just picked up the child and left. He was a very demanding man and an abusive drunk. Though Stanwyck divorced him, the Catholic Church did not recognize the divorce.

Betty was crazy about Frank. They were married in a civil ceremony but, because of his Catholicism, he continued to regard Stanwyck as his true wife.

Frank made Betty quit *Call Me Mister*. They had a beautiful baby girl and named her Deedee. Frank wouldn't let Betty wear makeup and controlled her friendships. Betty and Danny Kaye were good friends, but one night in Rueben's, Frank stopped her from talking to him.

He gave orders to the doorman in his building not to let me in to see the baby. His excuse to Betty was that I was going out with "an agent he loathed at MCA." I tearfully explained my dilemma to my friend Lucy and she said, "I'll get in. Come on!"

The famous redhead marched me over there and told the door-man in no uncertain terms to "Go to hell." Lucy and I saw the baby.

Lucy and Desi had not had children yet and she really made a fuss over baby Deedee.

Frank was not drinking anymore but sometimes a dry drunk is more abusive than a wet one. If Betty had a drink, she would chew coffee beans to disguise the fact, but the accusations still came. She said it was like being put on the witness stand.

The final break came over how their daughter Deedee would be brought up. After Betty left him, she received no financial support and he made no move to see Deedee again.

When Betty and I were appearing at the Roxy in New York, we brought Deedee up on stage during an afternoon performance. She was about three and the cutest doll you ever saw. Unknown to us, Frank was in the audience and saw her. He didn't let us know he was there, but later called Betty backstage to tell her what a good job she had done with their daughter. That was the last time we heard from him.

Years later, I was at a party for Jackie Gleason where I overheard George Burns, Milton Berle, Walter Matthau, Bob Newhart and Gleason discussing whom they considered the top monologist of their era. Every-one agreed it was Frank Fay.

When he died, he left all of his considerable estate to the Catholic Church. Frank and Barbara's adopted son, whom Barbara had long since disowned for bad behavior, resurfaced. He contested the will and won the entire estate.

Betty refused to hire an attorney to pursue what was rightfully Deedee's. Even Barbara Stanwyck advised her to do so. Betty was either too proud or too foolish.

Though Betty married again, I believe Deedee always felt deprived of her real father. When she was still little, she used to say, "Why doesn't Daddy want to see me?" How does one answer a question like that?

Frank Fay in Harvey

Betty Kean Fay and daughter, Deedee

With niece, Deedee, age eight, in Las Vegas

Jane and Betty Kean with Danny Kaye

The Kean Sisters

I was offered the starring role vacated by Betty Garrett in the Broadway company of *Call Me Mister*. At the same time, my sister Betty was starring in the national company that was touring the country. Her company featured up-and-coming young actors Carl Reiner, Buddy Hackett and Bob Fosse. Harry Anger, our agent from GAC (ICM today), pointed out that it was most unusual for sisters to be starring in the same role in different companies at the same time. He suggested we get an act together. He guaranteed us a guest shot on the Ed Sullivan's *Toast of the Town* when we came up with something. A lot of people were teaming up at that time because of the success of Martin and Lewis but there was no sister team doing this kind of comedy act.

Harry got us that shot on *Toast of the Town* and a writer. Eli Basse wrote us an eleven-minute act. Sullivan let us do the entire eleven minutes, which was a big deal. No single act generally got that much time. From that exposure we got many offers. All of the top clubs wanted us…Chez Paree in Chicago, Copa in New York, The Sands in Las Vegas. That was the time when nightclubs were really nightclubs and the acts were well-paid. We needed lots more material and Eli delivered. He was terrific and we were a hit.

> "…Exponents of high class, low comedy, their delivery
> is different, timely, bright and breezy slick slapstick…"
> — Gene Knight, *Daily News*

I hadn't thought of doing the act permanently because I loved doing legit theater. But, Betty and I were on the rise. The Kean Sisters played the top nightclubs in America and were booked into Vegas two or three times a year. We played beautifully off each other. We were such opposite types. I was the sophisticated one and Betty was the real physical, anything-for-a-laugh one.

Like many teams and most siblings, we had a number of disagreements during the eight years we worked together. That's one reason why we always insisted on separate dressing rooms. One night, while we were doing a tabloid version of *Make Mine Manhattan* at the Strand Theater in New York, Harry Anger came backstage to discuss booking the revue at the Beverly Club, a gaming nightclub in Kentucky. Because of the cost of transporting the show, he wanted to cut expenses and our salary. He approached Betty first and her first response was, "It's okay with me but you'd better ask Jane."

Then Betty quickly ran down to my dressing room and said, "Harry's going to ask us to take a cut! Say no!!" And she slipped quickly away.

When Harry came in and made his proposal, I replied, "It really isn't plausible. It's more expensive on the road. We'll have two rents, fares, wardrobe…"

Harry answered, "Well, Betty okayed it."

"She did?"

"She did."

"Well, let her do it then," I said. "I can't afford it."

So, Harry paid me $500 more a week.

After that, Betty always wanted me to handle the negotiations. Agents used to say, "Betty's easy to do business with, but that Jane is *tough!*"

We had an engagement at the Dunes in Las Vegas with Howard Keel. It was such a successful combination that Jules Podell booked both acts into the Copacabana in New York. Jules Podell reminded everyone of a heavy in a gangster movie. After the first show, Jules was sitting at a small table on the balcony drinking his fourth scotch when Howard Keel walked by.

Howard said, "Good evening, Mr. Podell."

"Can you take some constructive criticism?" Podell inquired.

"Of course, Mr. Podell," Howard answered.

"Go f— yourself," and Jules turned his attention back to his scotch.

We tried to explain Podell to Howard but he was devastated. Podell had a good side, if you went on a treasure hunt to find it. He had been known to help out his stars like Sammy Davis, Jr. who once came to him with financial problems. In doing so, he was guaranteed their exclusivity.

During this engagement, Jackie Gleason was appearing on stage at the La Vie Parisianne with the orchestra he'd put together. One night while Betty and I were performing, he paraded the entire band across the Copa floor causing quite a riot. Jackie made some lovely romantic albums using that orchestra with its huge string section and Bobby Hackett on the trumpet.

"South America, Take It Away" from Call Me Mister

Eli Basse, Tony Farrell, Jane, Jules Podell, Betty, and Jule Styne

Opening Night at Ciro's

With Ben Gage and Esther Williams

Jane and Betty with Christine Jorgensen after he/she went to Denmark for a sex change

With Groucho

Strand Theater, New York

Johnnie Ray

Betty and I met Johnnie at the Copacabana when he was the headliner and we were the supporting act. His performance on opening night was the most exciting thing I'd ever seen. He had that audience rocking from start to finish. His closing song was a spiritual, "I'm Gonna Walk and Talk with the Lord." There are few, in my opinion, who gave that much emotionally and dramatically. Before the show, my mother noticed him in a phone booth praying. She said, "He has a direct line to God!"

That night, there were people in the audience who were not the usual Copa goers…The Duchess of Windsor, Noel Coward, and Bette Davis. Yul Brynner, the star of *The King and I*, was there with Marlene Dietrich, as were newlyweds Frank Sinatra and Ava Gardner.

In between shows, Johnnie loved to do improvisations with his guests in his suite at the Fourteen Hotel next to the Copa. Everyone gladly accommodated him. He was now the toast of New York.

The dressing rooms at the Copa were totally inadequate, so it was necessary for the headliners to rent a suite at the Fourteen Hotel next door. It worked out well since the hotel elevator went directly to the Copa kitchen. Johnnie became such a good friend he even baby-sat with two-year-old Deedee while we did a club date at the Waldorf Astoria.

Johnnie and I were often listed as an item in the various columns. We went to openings together and posed for many publicity photos. Some items indicated that he'd proposed to me and I'd accepted him. We did love each other but more like brother and sister.

One night, Johnnie and I were at a party in New York and people were talking about Isabel Bigley who was playing the sweet girl in *Guys and Dolls*. Isabel was about to marry one of the heads of MCA and someone said she was still a virgin. Tallulah Bankhead spoke up with, "Doesn't her cherry get in the way when she f—s?!"

Tallulah was such a lady.

Johnnie became involved with Dorothy Kilgallen, the *New York Journal* columnist. She fell madly in love with him. The three of us used to go to all the nightspots together. At the beginning of their affair, I was the "beard" for them. After about a year, they threw caution to the wind and didn't care what anyone thought.

One year, she had a progressive birthday party for him. She hired a bus to take Johnnie's celebrated friends to a different four-star restaurant for every course. We wound up at El Morocco at two o'clock in the morning for dancing and more champagne.

One night shortly after that, Dorothy's husband, Dick Kollmar, came home and found them in a compromising position. He told Johnnie, "If I ever find you with my wife again, I'll kill you!" This scared the hell out of Johnnie and he refused to see or speak to her.

Johnnie showed me letters from Dorothy in which she pleaded with him to see her. Johnnie knew the friendship had gotten way out of control and was terrified of Kollmar. The irony was, Kollmar was always known to be a player. It was the same old story: It's okay if I do it, but you must not!

After numerous phone calls, he finally relented and they would see each other secretly. Dorothy was very good to him and, when he was deathly ill in a New York hospital, she was by his side. Their affair went on for many years.

Johnnie lived close to the edge. He entertained constantly at his 63rd Street apartment. He had many hangers-on who would keep his glass full but not bother to see that he ever ate. He went down to skin and bones and finally collapsed one night. He was convinced he was going to die.

With the help of his good friend Bill Franklin, he stopped drinking. Dorothy hired a cook to prepare some nourishing meals for him. Gradually, he became strong enough to work.

Johnnie loved the stage. He and my sister did *Bus Stop* together in Bucks County. Betty suggested the part of Bo for him. It wasn't a triumph but he had a good time. He was very fond of Betty and she looked out for him. They were close friends.

He gave her a puppy. That dog grew up to be the size of Trigger. Every time I'd go over to see her, the dog knocked me right on my butt.

Johnnie remained totally unspoiled. Though he loved his success, he stayed true to his Oregonian roots. When he wrote his autobiography, he said that he only loved two women in his life, his ex-wife, Marilyn Morrison, and Jane Kean. He couldn't mention Dorothy because of Kollmar, but I'm convinced he truly loved her, too.

I loved you, too, Johnnie!

Jane with Johnnie Ray

Jane and Dorothy Kilgallen

Walter

*"Good evening, Mr. and Mrs. America and all the ships
at sea. Let's go to press!"*

When Betty and I were appearing at the Copacabana with Johnnie,
Walter Winchell came to see the show. He was with Sherman Billingsly,
famed owner of the Stork Club. Copa management put a table on the
floor for the famous pair because the place was jammed. As was tradition
in our act, Betty and I ended by introducing whatever celebrities were in
the audience. When Betty introduced Walter, he jumped up from the
table and said, "I'm going to tell the world about you!"

And that he did. The following morning he devoted the entire first
paragraph of his column to us. The last three lines read:

> "…The Kean sisters at the Kopakabana, the Keanest,
> Kleverest and the Kwaziest! Komics from Koast to
> Koast! (Oh! The poor fellow, which one got him?)"
> — Walter Winchell, *The Daily Mirror*

We called him at his office to thank him and he then invited us to join
him after our late show. At that time, it was his habit to cruise New York
each night monitoring police calls on his short wave radio. As we drove
through Harlem, I was warned not to put my head out the window, as
there were often stray bullets flying around.

Walter began the habit of stopping by the Copa every night to take us
with him. Betty eventually dropped out to spend more time with her then
romantic interest, our manager, Howard Hoyt. He was to be husband
number three…or maybe four…it's difficult to keep track.

Jack O'Brien of *The Journal American* and his pretty, saintly-looking wife, Bonnie began to ride with Walter and me. Jack was then quite buddy-buddy with Walter. Bonnie was so demure that no one dared use a four-letter word in front of her. That put a bit of a damper on our exciting rides. Before we'd go riding, we'd sometimes dance to the rumba band at the Copa. Walter was a wonderful dancer and we often cleared the dance floor. It wasn't long before the O'Briens dropped out and that's when it all began. We became lovers.

He often read me his column before it came out and invited me to tell him about a friend or a place that I liked. Many times my preferences would appear in print. I suddenly became very popular with those who thought I could do something for them.

I had a small penthouse at 40 Central Park South, which I shared with my mother. Walter lived at the St. Moritz Hotel. The two buildings were divided by Rumplemayers, which became our morning rendezvous. I love the mornings and was generally up by about 10:30. Walter had trouble sleeping so we might meet for breakfast or lunch depending on how late he slept.

My mother liked Walter a great deal but she constantly reminded me of his marital status. It was difficult to think of him as a married man. Before we became acquainted, I remember him always with an empty seat beside him at the theater on opening nights. It wasn't long before I filled that seat.

He never tried to conceal our relationship. I was the one who was self-conscious about it. There would always be those people who thought I was using him for his journalistic clout. The truth is, I was very much in love with him.

I only went to his penthouse at the St. Moritz one time. Though his wife did not live with him, it was not a comfortable place for me. On the way down in the elevator, we ran into the manager, John Mados. My embarrassment was beyond words.

My terrace at 40 Central Park South was our favorite trysting place. It was very large and had a view of the city that was breathtaking. Those nights on the terrace were incredibly romantic but we never got too crazy because Mother was inside.

Betty and I were on the road a lot at the time. We were booked at the Chez Paree in Chicago, in Hollywood at The Mocambo and numerous stints in Las Vegas.

Before we opened our engagement at the Sands Hotel in Vegas in 1955, we went with Jimmy Durante to catch a few shows. The custom of the performers at the time was to arrive a few days early and see what the other acts were doing.

First we went to see the show at the Dunes. On the bill was a novelty act we had worked with in Chicago. It was a clever act that featured four ponies. We noticed there were only three in the act that night. When we went backstage to see the man whose act it was, he informed us that one of the ponies had escaped from its stall the night before and he hadn't been able to find it. He was very upset.

As Jimmy, Betty and I drove back to the hotel in the cab, we spotted the pony wandering near the road. We told the cab to stop and we got out to try and catch it. Now Betty had a bit to drink so this was quite a scene. When we finally caught the animal, Betty tried to calm it down saying, "Remember us? We worked with you in Chicago?"

I believe Betty may have been the first Horse Whisperer.

We were able to walk the pony back to the Dunes, through the Casino to the stage entrance. Not a soul looked up from the gambling tables.

The guy who lost his pony was elated. We drove on with Jimmy to catch Louis Prima at the Sahara. What a ball Las Vegas was then.

Whenever we were away from New York, Walter's secretary would send an advance copy of his column. At the top of the column Walter would frequently write me a love poem and sign it "Don Wahn." If he was trying to make me miss him, it worked.

When Betty and I opened a two-week gig at Ciro's in Hollywood, The Nicholas Brothers were our opening act and they really knew how to warm up an audience. That night, Walter threw a party for Louella Parsons and invited every top star, producer and newspaper columnist in Hollywood. Louella enjoyed the same power on the West coast that Walter enjoyed on the East coast. Marilyn Monroe, Betty Grable, Esther Williams, Groucho Marx, Danny Thomas, Danny Kaye, Lucy and Desi, Mickey Rooney, Donald O'Connor and many other greats were in attendance. Danny Kaye introduced us and I must say we brought the house down and received a standing ovation. The entire two weeks were sold out every performance. George Schlatter was the public relations man there at the time.

One night, I was dancing with Ron Fletcher between shows and Walter became so jealous that he kicked down the door on his way out. The following night, they put up a sign saying, "Through this door went the foot of Walter Winchell."

Louella Parsons wrote:

"…Some wise Hollywood producer could have a female Martin and Lewis in this clever comedy duo…"

When we returned a year later, she wrote:

"Betty and Jane Kean, those good looking comediennes are panicking audiences at the Mocambo…"

Next stop was the Palladium in London. While we were overseas, there was a cable from Walter outside my hotel room door every morning. Before we opened at the Palladium, we had a small banana crisis. We were informed that London was experiencing a shortage of bananas and we needed them for one of the best numbers in the act. Just before the show opened, we were visited by a representative from a foreign embassy bearing a bunch of bananas. The note said: Sent on the request of Walter Winchell.

We always incorporated impressions into our act and Walter suggested using Churchill's cigars for one of our bits, but the British P.H. department balked at that. We were a huge hit at the Palladium, which thrilled Walter and he had to quote a review from a London paper.

> "…Betty & Jane Kean, comedy duo, made a top im-
> pact with a standout routine. Their fast-paced clown-
> ing earned them a standing ovation at the closing half
> of the bill…"

Opening night at the Palladium remains to this day one of the most thrilling experiences in the theater that I ever had. I'm sure Betty felt the same way, too. The British are so enthusiastic and loyal. They never forget you. A photograph of Betty and me adorns the walls of the Palladium to this day.

When we returned from London, darling Walter had a photographer at the airport to take a photo for the middle section of *The Mirror*.

Upon my return, the romance continued with candlelit dinners at romantic places, dancing at the clubs and joyous lovemaking. He was extremely jealous and kept track of my every move. He even called me at the cleaners once when Mother told him I was there.

Walter told me that he had confessed his love for me to his pal Sherman

Billingsly, at the Stork Club one night. Sherman advised him to ask for a divorce, if he was that much in love. When he did, June replied, "After all I went through with you! Do you think I'm going to just hand you over to her now! No way!"

I believed him.

June bought a house in Phoenix, Arizona. Walter took no interest in the purchase. He was a New Yorker. What would he do there?

Eventually, he died there.

Walter loved spending the winter months or part of them in Miami Beach at the Roney Plaza Hotel. Betty and I worked there a lot during that time and we stayed at the Roney as well. Those winter months were truly wonderful. It was easy to see one another after the show and dine together. My mother was traveling with us. She never suspected I was "going all the way," as she called it. If she knew, she was in denial.

Believe me, she wouldn't have encouraged the romance had she known. I believe that her object in life was to keep me the village virgin. She never told me anything about sex except "don't let any man near you or you'll get pregnant!" The stigma of unwanted pregnancy was what an unmarried girl feared most and my mother played off of that fear.

Betty and I were appearing at the Latin Quarter in Miami Beach and having great success.

> "...The Kean Sisters have an act of action, of sight
> and sound which is jammed full of the kind of non-
> sense which makes for continuous laughter. Whatever
> Lou Walters is paying them, they're worth more!"
> — Paul Bruin, *Miami News*

I don't remember Lou giving us any raise!

There was an after-hours club across from the Roney called Murray Franklin's Lounge. We used to go there often after our show to hear a wonderful singer named Roberta Sherwood. Roberta was around fifty years old, always wore glasses and a sweater thrown over her shoulders. She sang with great feeling and we were all crazy about her. Walter went on a campaign to promote her. He got her an agent and she was finally recognized as the great talent that she was. Roberta never forgot his kindness. She was one of the few who called him at Cedars Sinai when he was dying of cancer.

Rowan and Martin were playing at a third-rate hotel on the beach in Miami at that same time. They were virtually unknown. I had seen them in Las Vegas at a hotel downtown and thought they were funny, so I asked Walter to take me to see them. When the hotel manager saw the great Winchell walk in, he invited everyone in the lobby to come to the show for free. Rowan and Martin were terrific and Walter launched another campaign. When Dan Rowan wrote his book, he mentioned my part in this incident. It was very nice of him to remember.

Whenever we were in New York, there were many great parties to attend. We went to one for Joe DiMaggio in the upstairs room at Toot Shor's. Joe was married to Marilyn Monroe at the time and I ran into her in the ladies room. She was in quite a state of distress. The chair she was sitting on had collapsed in a million splinters beneath her and left quite a number of them in her famous behind. She asked me sweetly if I would help her get them out. The dress was so tight, she could hardly pull it up and when she did, she had nothing on under it. I was working on a difficult splinter when Earl Wilson's wife, Rosemary, walked in. What a strange picture we must have made. Had Earl been with *The Enquirer* rather than *The New York Post*, I'm sure we would have made the front page the next day.

But Rosemary was a good sport and she ended up assisting me in the repair of Miss Monroe's behind.

That was my introduction to Marilyn.

Sometime later, Walter invited her to have dinner with Betty and me before we opened at Ciro's. I was planning to do an impression of her and he wanted to be sure she wouldn't be offended.

"Oh, that's all right," she cooed. "Lana Turner has been doing me for years."

Walter helped raise the money for the Broadway musical *Ankles Aweigh* in 1955. The show had a score by Sammy Fain and a book by Guy Bolton and Danny Shapiro. Rodgers & Hammerstein and 20th Century-Fox were investors. The money was raised in two weeks.

Betty and I were co-starred with featured actors Lew Parker, Gabriel Dell and Thelma Carpenter. Tony Charmoli did the choreography and staged some show-stopping dance routines.

Jerome Robbins came to New Haven to make some changes. I remember him asking us to do the soft shoe number to the "Eleven O'Clock Song." When we finished, he said, "That happens to be the routine I staged in *High Button Shoes*." He was right. A dancer we knew who was in *High Button Shoes* taught it to us. I've been doing the same routine ever since. I just changed the song.

The show was a tremendous hit in New Haven and Boston and completely sold out every performance. When we opened on Broadway, we had seven show-stopping rounds of applause during the show, but when the reviews came out, the critics never mentioned that. They just blasted us. Many felt we got slammed because Walter plugged it so much before it opened.

He had defied the critics before when he made *Hellzapoppin'* such a hit but Walter had all the enemies born of jealousy and envy that any powerful man has.

The show was a huge hit with audiences in spite of the initial reviews and it was amazing how the other columnists and celebrities got behind it figuring we didn't get a fair break. One columnist wrote:

> "The scandal of the week...the critical abuse of the talented people in *Ankles Aweigh*...great fun for the audience..."

Because of the initial reviews, *Ankles* was still not doing the business it should so Tony Farrell, who owned the Mark Hellinger Theater, took over the production reigns of the show. He called a meeting of the cast and suggested that, if everyone would be willing to take minimum wage, he would keep the show running through the hot summer months and, hopefully, it would get on its feet.

Betty and I had a meeting with our agents from William Morris who felt the show didn't have that much of a chance, under the circumstances. They had bookings on the club circuit and in Las Vegas at healthier salaries. They advised us to leave. Betty and I agreed and told Tony we'd be quitting the show at the end of the week. It looked as though they would have to close.

As usual, Betty and I had dressing rooms at opposite ends of the stage. While I was packing my things, I heard a cheer come from the stage and the stage manager knocked on my door. He told me to leave my shoes for my understudy who would be going on in my place Monday night. When I asked what had happened, he informed me that Betty had agreed to stay. With my exit, they could give her more money.

Betty was staying?! We were co-stars! We were a team!!

I felt completely betrayed. Suddenly, I was the heavy and Betty was the hero. If she had told me she was in love with Lew Parker and wanted to stay, I might have understood.

When Walter picked me up at the theater that night, he was as shocked as I was. He took a very sad sister home.

I wanted desperately to get away, so I called various airlines to try and book a flight to Europe. I had never been to the continent and it seemed to be just the thing to cure the blues. It was summer and tourist travel was heavy. All European flights were booked.

I told Walter of my predicament and, the next day, a representative from TWA came to my apartment with two first-class tickets. I started to write a check but was told they were compliments of Howard Hughes.

My mother wouldn't fly, Betty and I weren't speaking, and I didn't have a single friend who was free to join me. I turned the second ticket in and went to Europe alone.

I arrived in Rome, not understanding a word of Italian and already regretting the whole thing. As I stood in the center of the terminal, feeling terribly sorry for myself, my name came out over the loudspeaker. Mr. Hughes had arranged for a limo to take me to the Excelsior Hotel. With that kind of treatment, I was determined I couldn't stay depressed.

It was a funny feeling, being alone in a foreign country. I met some Americans in Rome who invited me to join them in Cannes. They were able to get invitations to the Gala in Monte Carlo where Danny Kaye was scheduled to appear.

At the Gala, I sighted one of the most gorgeous men I have ever seen and pointed him out to my friend.

"Oh, that's Prince Ranier III," she said.

I met the Prince who was charming and dashing. This was shortly before he was captured by Grace Kelly.

As I walked through the Casino after the show, I stumbled on Danny Kaye and his wife, Sylvia Fine, who was responsible for a lot of his success. She was bawling him out like he was a twelve-year-old. He hadn't done the numbers she told him to do and he laid a big egg. Bits he had chosen to do did not translate well to the mostly French audience. Sylvia was furious. I ducked away unseen.

I traveled abroad for six weeks and, when I returned, I had to get ready to do the engagements to which Betty and I had already committed.

When we opened at the Latin Quarter in 1955, Walter wrote:

"…Jane Kean and her former sister, Betty, are opening at the Latin Quarter on Nov. 26th…"

We could always hide our differences on stage but off-stage, things were very tense. After *Ankles Aweigh*, my trust in my sister was shaken. It was a depressing sight to see my name taken off that marquee.

Beside the conflict with Betty, I was having a major one with my mother over my relationship with Walter. She was aware that he could never get a divorce and felt I was throwing away any chance for a future happiness with someone else. It was disturbing her to such an extent that I finally felt I had to break up with him. As usual, she had the last word. As much as I hated it, I knew she was right.

I met Walter at Rumplemayers and broke the news. I tearfully explained the futility of our relationship and how much it was upsetting Helen. He did not take it well. He was convinced I was seeing someone else. That couldn't have been further from the truth. I was still very much in love with him.

A friend of mine once said to me, "A love that ends while still it lives will never, ever die."

My love was far from dead.

After I broke up with him, he never mentioned me in his column at all. I was in the cut dead department. Men were afraid to ask me out. They didn't want to get in Walter's bad graces. Whenever I ran into him at Rueben's or El Morocco, he wouldn't even speak to me.

There was only one guy who had the courage to take me out. George Gilbert, the producer of *Mr. Wonderful*, starring Sammy Davis, Jr. George didn't care what Walter thought. He was fun and a true friend.

One day about six months later, I bumped into Walter on 59th Street. I told him I didn't want us to be enemies. We had meant too much to each other. I explained again how our relationship was upsetting Helen. We talked for hours, and, after that, we became loving friends.

A few years later, Walter was narrating *The Untouchables* at Desilu. Lucy ran into him and told him that I was going to marry Dick Linkroum from NBC. He had the exclusive and he printed it on the second page of *The Daily Mirror*. That was Walter's way of saying congratulations.

Walter Winchell

Winchell always preferred being
photographed with his hat on

Choreographer Tom Hagan, Helen Kean, Jane, and Walter Winchell
at the Persian Room in New York

Winchell gave Jane her first dog, "Baybee," pictured here with Betty

The Kean Sisters at the Copacabana

With Durante and Liberace in Las Vegas

Jane, Marilyn, Milton Berle and Betty at Chasen's

The Kean Sisters en route to London's Palladium

*At Café de Paris in London with singer Al Martino, Paladium producer Val Parnell,
Noel Coward, Betty, and manager Dick Gabe*

"Walk Like a Sailor" from Ankles Aweigh

Playing the Palladium

Arriving from Europe on TWA

Me, Myself and I

After Betty and I went our separate ways, I hired choreographer Ron Fletcher to stage an act for me. Mother was very much behind this move and attended every rehearsal. Ron created a wonderful act. I wanted it to be totally different from what Betty and I did together so no one would compare the two. Originally, I planned to hire another boy dancer but I felt so good with Ron. After a bit of pleading, he agreed to perform with me. When the act was in good shape, I asked Sam Bramson of the William Morris office to have a look. He immediately got us a booking at the Eden Roc in Miami Beach.

> "…Jane Kean is breaking in her new act, without sister Betty. As far as we're concerned, Betty should get married more often and let Jane work by herself. She's got a production that can headline any classy supper club in the country…"
>
> — *Miami News*

Immediately after that we were booked into the Tropicana in Las Vegas.

> "…Jane Kean's act is classy and delightful from the intro when she walks out on a mink carpet, then smoothly plunges into a series of songs and devastating impressions. Miss Kean's material and gowns are all top level…"
>
> — *Variety*

The most challenging engagement had to be the Copacabana where Betty and I had enjoyed such success. I was worried until the reviews came out:

> "…Brilliant Jane Kean shines in new show at the Copacabana. I think this is one of the most refreshing acts I've seen in a long time…"
> — Earl Wilson, *New York Post*

Home free!

One of the highest compliments I have ever received was from Jimmy Durante. Jimmy had seen my act at The Tropicana and requested me for his television special. When the network said they were over budget and refused, he said, "All right, I'll pay her out of my own pocket." And he did.

Lucy and Desi came to my opening at the Copa. They sent flowers and a congratulatory note. She nearly always attended my openings after that and was gracious about posing for publicity photos.

Ron and I were booked together with Rowan and Martin at The Chase Hotel in St. Louis and two return dates at The Eden Roc with Alan King. Immediately after that, Ron had to leave to choreograph the Ice Capades. Rather than replace him, I decided to return to the Broadway stage.

I was offered the lead replacing Jayne Mansfield in *Will Success Spoil Rock Hunter?* Jayne would do anything to get publicity. One time, she appeared on top of the Paramount Building in a bikini in the middle of December. When I took over for the bosomy Miss Mansfield, Jack Carter sent me a telegram saying, "You'll be bigger than Mansfield…Irving, that is!"

On opening night I was sent flowers in which prankster friends had concealed a pair of falsies. How gauche!

I was expected to perform the same type of publicity stunts that Jayne had. When I was asked to do a layout for *Esquire*, the photographer wanted me to show much more than I was willing to. The poor man was so disappointed when I only allowed him to reveal my legs and a bit of cleavage.

Rock Hunter went well until one performance when I kept Martin Gabel waiting on stage for what he thought was an eternity. I saw a huge rat in my dressing room and I wouldn't put my feet down.

Apparently, Jayne used to come in at the last minute before curtain, borrow a comb from someone, and dash on. One night, no one would loan her one, so she used a fork. What a character.

Everyone liked Jayne with the exception of Mae West. Jayne stole Mickey Hargitay away from the fabulous Ms. West. He was one of the six muscle men Mae used in her nightclub act.

Tom Poston was also in *Rock Hunter* and great fun to work with. Although the show closed after a short run, I got to deliver what continues to be one of my favorite lines: "Everybody thinks of me as a sex symbol. I'm not that way at all. I'm just horrible in bed. Everybody says so!"

George Axelrod could really write comedy. Too bad he's no longer with us.

Next I did *The Pajama Game* at the New York City Center followed by *Happy Hunting* at the Starlight Theater in Kansas City. The Starlight was a wonderful open-air theater with the capacity to seat over 5,000 people.

My leading man, Bill Hayes, normally took his keynote from an instrument in the orchestra. One particular night a train whistle screamed at the exact same time and Bill accidentally took his note from that. It was three keys higher. I was no help at all because I couldn't stop laughing.

People frequently came to the Starlight equipped with raincoats because it sometimes rained. The show was supposed to continue rain or shine. I remember during my opening number it started to pour. I mean a cloudburst. I continued to sing, with my eyelashes coming off and makeup running down my face. The song was "Gee, But It's Good To Be Here." It wasn't. They finally had to stop and give the audience rain checks.

A new act with Ron Fletcher

On the ten best dressed list

Glamour photo

Will Success Spoil Rock Hunter? *photo for* Esquire *magazine, 1961*

Summer With Dan

I went on tour in the play *Burlesque*, starring Dan Dailey. There were several dance numbers added to the old script so Dan could show his expertise and I got to dance with him. A challenge if I ever saw one. Elliot Norton, the dean of legit critics, thrilled me with his review:

> "…Jane Kean acts with Dan in *Burlesque*, and gives a fine performance. She lights up the play with the honest warmth of her acting…"
>   — Elliot Norton, *Boston Globe*

I felt like Sally Field… "You like me, you really like me!"

Dan was one of my favorite actors and musical performers. He was one of Lucy's favorites, too. She loved his performance in *When Willie Comes Marching Home*, and used to play the film for friends when she entertained.

Dan started out as an actor under contract to MGM but had better opportunities when he signed with 20th Century-Fox as a dancer. There, they teamed him up with Betty Grable and other blondes at the studio.

I learned to dance a soft shoe with him and it was pure joy. In one poignant scene, Dan's character breaks down when his wife Bonnie (my part) leaves him because of his drinking. Dan's performance never failed to bring tears to my eyes.

His drinking wasn't only done on stage. He had an ice tub full of beer backstage and would consume the whole tub before the curtain came down.

I was very fond of Dan and we became very close during the run of the show. When we returned to New York, he wanted to continue seeing me. He said his wife Gwen was divorcing him.

I decided to check this out before I went any further with him. I was acquainted with Gwen from the days when she was married to Donald O'Connor, so I invited her to lunch at Toots Shors. When I asked her if it was true, she confirmed their split. I then asked if she had a problem with my dating Dan and she said, "I couldn't care less."

Dan and I started seeing each other very seriously. He managed to cut down on his drinking and we had great fun. We went dancing at El Morocco and The Stork Club. We hit every glamorous nightclub in New York.

Dan was very romantic. Our relationship was developing beautifully until he went to Europe to do a show. His European company consisted of heavy drinkers like Ann Sheridan, Scott McKay and Myron McCormick. That was the end of his sobriety and, ultimately, our relationship.

Before he left, I received a telegram from Gwen saying, "I'm sending Dan's *skirts and sweaters* to you. I'm sure you can get them to him quicker than I can."

Dan had been reported to like prancing around in women's clothes but I never saw that side of him. He was all man with me. Or, maybe my clothes wouldn't fit him. He was awfully tall.

A Mother's Choice

My life took a dramatic turn when my mother discovered she had breast cancer. She refused to see a doctor or go to a hospital. She wouldn't even let me hire a nurse and she forbade me to tell anyone of her condition. For some reason, it was important to her to keep quiet about it.

For a long time, she lived as she always had. She continued to dress up and put on makeup so the few guests that came to the apartment were completely unaware of her condition.

A maid was also out of the question, so I was nurse, cook and housekeeper.

Monte Proser called me to headline a revue he was producing for the El Rancho Hotel in Las Vegas. Eli Basse was on board to write it, so I was guaranteed good material.

I was very hesitant about accepting this job because I was so worried about my mother. She still would not let me get any help yet she insisted I take the Las Vegas engagement. She said it was too good to turn down. She would order room service from Rumplemayers. She would be fine.

I confided in my niece, Deedee, and asked her to check in on Helen after school. Deedee was my confidante then and still is today.

Las Vegas was hopping. The Rat Pack was appearing at the Sands Hotel at night and filming *Ocean's Eleven* during the day. Frank and the gang came to see my late show. They were very enthusiastic and invited me to join them at the Silver Slipper where Hank Henry and a burlesque show were playing. The late show didn't go on until 4 a.m. so we got out at 5:30. They went straight to the set of *Ocean's Eleven*. I went straight home to bed.

Betty and I had worked with Joey Bishop at the Chez Paree in Chicago and Sammy and I were good friends. Dean Martin was also an old buddy. I worked with him when he was a band singer at the Hollenden Hotel in Cleveland. That was BNJ…before nose job. I had met Frank when I played the Copa and he was apparently impressed by my act. One night, as I passed by his corner table, he said, "You have a mother f——— act." That was high praise from Frank.

I called Mother twice a day and she always assured me she was fine. About three months into the engagement, I panicked one day when she didn't answer the phone. I promptly informed Beldon Katleman, owner of El Rancho, that I had to leave. He offered me more money and all kinds of perks if I would stay but I refused. Rhonda Fleming replaced me and I returned to New York to be with my mother.

Helen was obviously worse but still insisted she was okay. She still refused to go to the hospital. Late one night, I had a premonition and went into her room. I laid down on the bed next to her holding her hand. The next morning she was gone.

She never lapsed into a coma and never once requested a painkiller.

I immediately got in touch with Betty and Lew Parker, who were married by then, and called Daddy in Syracuse. Lew was wonderful. He came right over and took care of all the details. I held up well aside from the sight of her going out in a body bag. It all seemed like a bad dream.

The service was simple, as my mother had requested. Our friends remembered her with dozens of beautiful flower arrangements. Anyone who knew the Kean sisters knew Helen.

Taking apart Helen's sick bed was a horrible chore until I discovered thirty thousand dollars in cash under the mattress. Mother always took care of my finances and she didn't have much faith in banks. I did, however, and promptly deposited the find.

My father passed away one year later. They were never divorced.

The "Rat Pack" and friends. Standing with Jane, left to right: Marty Ingels, Dean Martin, Patrice Wymore (Errol Flynn's widow), Frank Sinatra, Sammy Davis, Jr., Joey Bishop, Hank Henry.

Life After Helen

After my mother passed away, I had a call from Lucy inviting me to visit her and Desi in Palm Springs. They were having a Halloween party. The change might be just what I needed. Lucy knew better than anyone how close I had been to Helen.

I flew to Palm Springs and my date for Lucy's Halloween party was George Maharis. Lucy knew I had a crush on him. He later became very hot, starring on the show *Route 66*. He couldn't have been cuter. We danced and he made me laugh but our relationship never went any further than that night.

A few years later, we resumed our friendship in Sacramento in 1962. We were both appearing in a production of *Guys and Dolls*. George made a great Sky Masterson.

When Lucy and Desi went back to Beverly Hills they invited me to stay in their charming little guesthouse at 1000 Roxbury Drive. Lucy thought I should advise my agents at William Morris that I was going to be on the West Coast for a while and they should find me work in California. It wasn't long before they did.

Typical New Yorker, I didn't know how to drive. I had to rely on Lucy or her driver, Frank, to get anywhere. Lucy used to insist I go with her to the beauty parlor. I'd sit for hours waiting for her to get a comb out. It was at that time, I realized I'd have to learn to drive or go back to New York.

The final straw came when I neglected to call a cab after an interview in Hollywood and started walking. My heels were killing me. Finally, a cute guy in a convertible stopped and I asked him to take me to the nearest rent-a-car place. I suspect I disappointed him. There was a motel only three blocks away.

I rented a blue Falcon. Thanks to Walter's influence, I had already obtained a license that I simply used as identification. I had only actually driven a car one other time and that had been a catastrophe. Though I had vowed never to drive again, it was now a necessity. The whole thing looked simple enough…put the car in drive and put your foot on the brake at the red light. I nosed the Falcon onto Wilshire Boulevard and crept home going about five miles an hour.

By now, I had moved into my own apartment and I pulled the car into the garage there. The next morning, I realized I would have to back the car out. This new challenge was beyond my novice skills. I smacked the car into the garage wall and was forced to call Lucy and ask Frank to come over and get me out of the driveway. After only one more rescue by Frank, I became the Barney Oldfield of West Hollywood.

I was sorry to see Lucy split with Desi, but I know she had a good reason because she loved him dearly. And how she loved those children. She was a good mother. Whenever she was in New York, she called them often, to check on what they were doing.

"Desi, did you take your drum lesson today?" she'd say. She believed in tough love. She sent me pictures of them when they were little. They were so adorable.

After the divorce, she decided to make a dramatic move. She furnished a stunning apartment on New York's East side and did a musical called *Wildcat*. Cy Coleman played the score for us one day and the songs were really good. Lucy had never done a musical on stage before and though she had a vocal coach, the eight shows a week took a toll on her voice. They closed the show down for two weeks while she recuperated. That was unfortunate because it was selling out. After that, the show lost its momentum. It was during that show that she met Gary Morton. She began to laugh again. I was an usher at Norman Vincent Peal's church for their wedding. It was the first time I'd ever heard applause at the end of the ceremony. She gave up the apartment in New York, gave all the lovely furniture to her mom, and bought her a house in Brentwood to put it in. Is that class or what?!

When Lucy and I first met, she said, "I'll be your friend for life." She was.

In Las Vegas before animal rights with Lucy

George Maharis and Jane in Guys and Dolls *in Sacramento, 1962*

Little Lucy and Little Desi

With Lucy and manager Marty Goodman

The Landlady

I was quite happy in my first Hollywood apartment. It was furnished with scattered antiques along with other items from the old Akron, comparable now to Pier One. I became very friendly with my landlady, Peggy. She had a grande dame demeanor and boasted about her early film career and her association with Gloria Swanson. Peggy owned three apartment buildings, two on Doheny Drive and one on Norton.

I was called to New York by David Merrick to pinch hit for Kaye Ballard who was taking a five-week hiatus from *Carnival* starring Anna Maria Alberghetti and staged by Gower Champion. When I returned from New York, my charming landlady had moved me out and into the building she owned on Norton Avenue in West Hollywood.

I was stunned but I couldn't stay angry with her because the apartment had a baby grand and was really very nice. I still had trouble believing that she would pack up all my stuff and move me, but she had an offer she couldn't refuse on my old apartment.

Shortly after that episode, Peggy called me, "A charming man just rented one of my apartments, the one next to Marilyn Monroe's. I think you should meet him. He's from New York and is going to work for Burt Leonard at Screen Gems. He might be able to get you on a show." She invited us both to dinner.

As soon as Dick Linkroum walked in the room, I knew I was going to marry him. He was brilliant, with a personality that wouldn't quit, tall and lean with gray hair and green eyes. Simply beautiful. We were married three weeks later in Tijuana. I couldn't understand a word of the ceremony, so a month later we did a retake at Los Angeles City Hall.

Before we were married, the infamous landlady, Peggy, tried to break us up because she was afraid she was going to lose two tenants. Peggy liked 100% occupancy. She would ask what I thought of Dick and, when I said I liked him, she would say, "Well, you know, he's very cheap." On the other side, she told Dick he could never afford me because I was so extravagant. She lost her tenants anyway.

For two and a half years, it was perfect bliss. We had one of those relationships where he'd come in the door and throw his arms around me. We were a TV romance. A real Ozzie and Harriet.

It was 1962 and a truly exciting time. Dick had been in television since its inception. He had directed a show in New York with Jack Lemmon and his then wife, Cynthia. He directed the first Jack Benny Show. He was a television whiz kid and now he was doing *Route 66*, and later *F Troop*, two of the hottest shows on television. We bought a home in Studio City. I became so domesticated that I completely lost interest in my career. I learned how to cook. I baked bread and made fancy desserts. We had a dog in the backyard and a mortgage. We entertained a lot. It wasn't like being out of the business because Dick brought so many of his associates home.

My niece, Deedee, came to visit from New York. She was about twelve years old at the time. One afternoon, as we enjoyed lunch on the terrace, Dick became stiff as a board and writhed in convulsions on the ground. He had told me he had epilepsy when we were married but it simply hadn't sunk in. The important thing to do, I'd been told, was to put something in his mouth, so he wouldn't swallow his tongue. I did this and then ran to my good friend and neighbor, John Marley (he played the producer who found the horse's head in his bed in *The Godfather*), and asked him to help me carry Dick to bed. Dick remained unconscious for a half hour or so. When he woke up, he was very sad and apologetic. He seemed so vulnerable. It only made me love him more.

He had experienced his first seizure at the age of 28 when he was still serving in the Navy. He had always been careful to tell those he worked with about his condition so they would know what to do in the event he had an attack. He took Delatin to control it. It had never affected his employment opportunities and he held many important positions at various networks.

I got a call from Screen Gems one day to pick him up after one of his seizures. After that, Dick wasn't able to obtain a driver's license until he could prove he hadn't had an occurrence for a year. I was happy to drive him around. I loved being needed. As soon as he obtained his license, I gifted him with a red fiat. He loved it!

We decided to install a pool in the backyard and had a wonderful time working on the house together. I went to the paint store one day and it was there I overheard the salesman saying that John F. Kennedy had been shot. I ran home to tell Dick. We stayed by the television the rest of the day following the heartbreaking details of the assassination.

I wanted desperately to get pregnant. When it looked like I couldn't, we began taking steps toward adoption. Many wonderful friends including Lucy and Desi wrote glowing letters of recommendation. We entered the final stages with the agency.

In June of our third year of marriage, I went to my niece's graduation in New York. I was gone about ten days, and when I came back, Dick seemed cool and not a bit happy to see me. The next morning, I awoke to see him walking out with suitcase in hand. I asked him where he was going and he said he had to be by himself for a while. It was nothing I'd done. He just needed time to think.

He checked into the Chateau Marmont and I didn't hear from him until a week later when he stopped by to tell me he was in love with someone else. He was then Vice President of United Artists in charge of television specials. He had become involved with his secretary. Such a cliché!

It was an incredible shock. I couldn't eat and began to lose weight. At least I got that out of it. The gal from the adoption agency came over to see the house. I explained that it was too late and told her what had happened. We would have to withdraw from the adoption. She was almost as surprised as I was. Having a child in the picture would have made the outcome even more painful. I guess it was a blessing in disguise.

Dick rented a house on Benedict Canyon and moved in with the secretary and her eight-year-old daughter by a previous affair. Two weeks later, he called and said he'd made a mistake. He loved me. Could he come home? I made the age-old mistake: I said yes.

I confided in my longtime friend, television actress, Jane Dulo. She had named Dick "Mr. Wonderful." She had been in analysis for eight years and could predict every move he made with amazing accuracy. She would say, "He'll call tomorrow." He would.

He came back for a week or so and then decided he couldn't live without the secretary. Back to Benedict Canyon. This went on for many months.

Finally, the secretary became pregnant. Dick asked me to divorce him in a Tijuana court. He said we could then go across the street and remarry.

He just wanted to give the child a name. I told him I would pass. The whole thing was an insult to my intelligence.

In the months that followed, we tried to reconcile. We took a trip by car stopping at Yellowstone, the Painted Desert and the Grand Canyon. Our final destination, New York. There we saw a few shows. The night we went to see *The Odd Couple* with Art Carney and Walter Matthau, I ran into an old agent of mine. He wanted to know where to get in touch with me in case something came up that was right for me.

Ten days later, we returned to California and there were several calls waiting for me. "You are going to play Art Carney's wife in the new *Honeymooners* series," my agent announced. I would have to leave for rehearsals in Miami right away. Dick wanted to accompany me to Florida and work on a book he'd had in mind for some time. We could continue to work on our marriage. We packed up and drove to Florida.

"Mr. Wonderful," Dick Linkroum

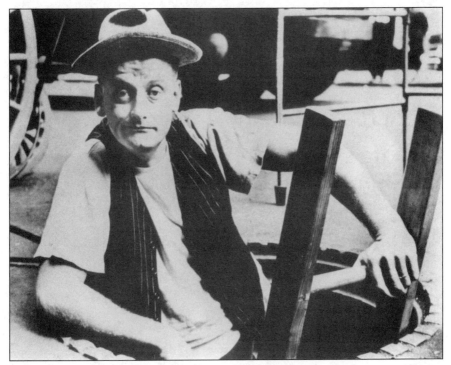

Art always emerged from the sewer—smelling like a rose!

Trixie and Ed Norton

Gleason And The Honeymooners

They say timing is everything in life and *The Honeymooners* came just at the right time for me. Jackie was so glad to see me and Art Carney was a doll. We all worked extremely well together.

Sheila MacRae was hired to play Alice. Her interpretation was very different from Audrey Meadows. She wanted to play it much softer. There was some dispute over this at the first rehearsal. Sheila said to Jackie, "My Alice cries." To which he replied, "Not on *this* show. If you don't come back and top me, the audience will hate me." He always took the curse off of yelling at Alice by saying, "Baby, you're the greatest."

CBS constructed a rehearsal studio adjoining the grounds of the country club so Jackie could drive over there in his golf cart. At that period, he was a big golf enthusiast. He had insisted on doing the show from Miami so he could play golf year round. He tried to interest everyone in the game but, of the entire group, I think only June Taylor stuck with it.

Things were also going well with Dick and me. We rented a great apartment, gave parties, and made new friends. Gleason producer Jack Philbin remembered Dick from his NBC days and Dick fit right in with the Gleason group.

I loved doing *The Honeymooners* that season. It was a thrill to be a part of a show so solid that it became number one. Dick was on his good behavior. His book, *One Before Bedtime*, was going well. After the six-month season, we returned home.

Back in Hollywood, Dick took a little office away from the house on Ventura Boulevard. It wasn't long before he came to me and asked if he could invite the old secretary and the new baby over to the house.

Please. Was he kidding?

I returned to Florida for the second season of *The Honeymooners*. We decided to rent out our house and just keep a small apartment in Hollywood. Dick would stay and continue to write and I'd fly home when I could.

The day before the first taping of the new season, I received a "Dear John" letter asking, once again, for a divorce. It said he had come to realize that his love for Lily was real and he wanted to marry her. I hired a lawyer and started proceedings.

Within days, I received another wire: "Stop divorce proceedings. I've made a terrible mistake."

It's almost funny now, but then it was a different matter. I didn't know which way to turn. This went on for another two years.

The last time, it was the Christmas holiday and he wanted to come to Miami. "Oh please, we belong together. I want to come down and be with you."

It was the last season of the weekly show. I had filed for divorce and it would be final in just a few months. This time I said no.

I was Dick's third wife. He never married the secretary but had a brief and torrid affair with Anne Baxter, the lovely actress from *All About Eve*. He finally married a writer and moved to Palm Springs.

Most people are aware that Jackie hated to rehearse. He had a photographic memory and was a quick study. Art stayed on the script until the last minute. We never used teleprompters. We all had to know the show cold by airtime. That was something Jackie insisted on. He didn't like retakes. He believed the audience wouldn't have the same response to a joke the second time around. I don't think we did a retake more than three times in five years.

One mistake I remember was made during a song Art and I sang together. His line was "Remember Cain, the guy who slew his brother." Art made a mistake and it came out "Remember Cain, the guy who blew his brother."

As we watched the tape in Jackie's dressing room, Art realized his mistake and insisted on re-doing it. Jackie's reaction was, "Oh, forget it. People will think they heard it wrong."

Art insisted on keeping the orchestra and redoing it. So, we did.

One particularly memorable show was when Pert Kelton guested on the show as Alice's mother. Pert originally created the role of Alice on *Cavalcade of Stars* with Gleason, and was wonderful. She had that natural twang in her voice, which Audrey later cultivated when she got the role. When Jackie moved to CBS from DuMont, CBS wouldn't hire Pert because she was blacklisted. She had been one of the unfortunates involved in Senator McCarthy's communist witch-hunt.

The rehearsals for the show were hilarious. How I wish I had tapes of the times when Jackie and Art ad-libbed. At airtime, they stuck strictly to the terrific dialogue that Marvin Marx, Walter Stone and Rod Parker wrote.

Jackie had a strong aversion to ethnic jokes, any sexual references or anything that was in bad taste. As funny as *All in the Family* was, Jackie would never have said some of the things Carroll O'Connor did. He was almost puritanical. At first readings, he would red pencil anything he considered risqué. He'd say to the writers, "You can't say that!", to which they'd reply, "But Jackie..." and that's as far as they would get. I can't imagine what he would say about what's said on television today.

During the show's four years, many changes took place in the private lives of *The Honeymooners'* cast.

At the end of the first season, Sheila married the producer of the show, Ronnie Wayne, a very personable guy who was mad for her. The marriage didn't last long. I think Gordon MacRae was a tough act to follow. And Ronnie couldn't sing.

Art's life changed when his first wife Jean divorced him and remarried. Art was very unhappy about this. It was evident he still had strong feelings for her.

Art returned from our Christmas hiatus married to Barbara Isaacs, a girl he had known for several years. She was a script girl with David Susskind and a very attractive brunette. She had always been crazy about Art and proceeded to try and make a happy life for him. They bought a co-op in Manhattan and she traveled with him to the West Coast when he did *Harry and Tonto*. Things looked good for a while but Art never really got over Jean. When he heard her second marriage didn't work out, and she was getting a divorce, he divorced Barbara so he and Jean could remarry.

I had the pleasure of seeing him, a few years ago, when I was in a musical version of the movie *Arthur* at the Goodspeed Opera House near their home in Westbrook, Connecticut. The stage manager came to me during rehearsal one day and said, "You have a guest in your dressing room."

It was Art. He and Jean came to see the show and then we had lunch together at their home. They showed me pictures of the children and grandchildren who lived in the next town. He seemed happy and expressed no wish to perform again.

Jackie's reunion with Genevieve didn't last. He really tried but there seemed to be too many differences. He soon fell in love with June Taylor's sister, Marilyn, who was one of June's dancers. When Jackie slipped and broke his leg on one of the shows, Marilyn visited him in the hospital. She was holding his hand when Genevieve walked in. It was apparently quite a scene. She knew they were in love but refused to consent to a divorce. The incident hit all the newspapers.

Marilyn picked up stakes and moved to Chicago where she met and married a businessman and had a son.

Jackie started dating another June Taylor dancer named Honey Merrill. They were together for about ten years and then amicably called it quits.

Jackie finally got a divorce when the divorce laws in New York changed. The new law stated that, if a couple lived apart for two years, he or she could get a divorce without the other's consent.

He met Beverly McKittrick on a golf course in Florida and married her after a brief courtship. I'm not sure why Jackie married so hastily, but the marriage was of short duration.

Marilyn came down to Florida to visit her sister after her husband passed away. Jackie called her and they started seeing each other again and eventually married. He never got over her. He was an incurable romantic.

We did the weekly show of *The Honeymooners* for four years, 1966 to 1970. During hiatus, Jackie would remain in Florida so he could golf while the rest of us returned to homes and family in New York or California.

After we became number one, Jackie lost some of his enthusiasm. He had been offered movie roles and he was ready to move on to other things. CBS would have liked to have had a season or two more. We all would have. But, Jackie had had it.

In a few years, he wanted to do a *Honeymooners* special. He got Audrey Meadows back and we did several of them. The last show was televised from the stage of the Resorts International Hotel in Atlantic City. We performed the same show in the nightclub there for the next six nights without changing a word. Every performance was sold out.

Jackie's Peekskill Production Company never sold *The Honeymooners* to London. That's amazing to me because Gleason and Carney did the kind of comedy that England loves.

With all the wonderful work Jackie did in the three mediums of stage, television and movies, he never received an Oscar or an Emmy, only a Tony award in 1959 for *Take Me Along* on Broadway. In September of 2000, however, the City of New York erected an eight-foot bronze statue of Jackie as the character Ralph Kramden at Port Authority Bus Station. I think Jackie would really have liked that. Bronze is so permanent.

Art and wife Barbara, 1967

Jane and husband Joe Hecht in Gypsy *in New Orleans in 1980, with "Chowsie" the wonder dog!*

The Great One

Art, Jane and Jean, 1990

Along Came Joe

While I was in Miami doing the last season of *The Honeymooners*, I stayed at The Racquet Club, a yacht and tennis club that also had suites. I had a gorgeous penthouse and, since we started taping in August, I got terrific off-season rates. Dick Linkroum was finally out of my life and I began to go out with Joe Hecht who was the managing director of the club.

In January 1970, I got the bill for my room and it was sky high…three thousand for the month! By now, Joe and I were very close, so I went to him and said, "What is this?"

Joe said, "Business is business. Season is here now and your suite gets $3000 during the season." I couldn't believe it. That was more than four times what I had been paying. Joe asked if I would like to get the suite for nothing and I said of course. He said, "Well, marry me then."

I always like to save money. So, I did.

Our wedding was held on a gorgeous yacht that had belonged to Ann Sothern. We had it decorated like a wedding chapel and sailed up to Fort Lauderdale. The wedding guests got off there and went back to Miami by a special bus. We stayed aboard and honeymooned. Gleason sent me a wire saying, "Anything that gets you away from Norton, including bigamy, is okay with me."

Everyone from *The Honeymooners* attended the wedding and many friends from California flew in to join us, including my darling Deedee.

There's a song that goes, "When your love is new and each kiss an inspiration…" It was a good beginning. Joe and I got an apartment overlooking the bay across from the club.

The Honeymooners came to a close and everyone connected with it went back to New York or California. That group had been like my family. Joe was busy working all day. I had three cats and that was it.

I played the dutiful wife and hostess at the club. They had a wonderful French chef and I had all my meals there. The weather was beautiful and that would have been enough if I had been ready to retire but I wasn't. I always considered Miami "God's waiting room." I was, frankly, lonesome and a little bored.

After several months, I took a trip to New York to check on my apartment on 55th Street. I had maintained it over the years and, whenever we had a break from *The Honeymooners*, I flew to New York to see the new shows and my friends.

While in New York, I was offered the role of Sally in the road tour of Stephen Sondheim's *Follies*. The cast consisted of Vivian Blaine, Robert Alda, Hildegarde, Lynn Bari, Selma Diamond, Julie Wilson and Mary Small. I hadn't seen Mary since *Early to Bed* but she seemed to have mellowed since then.

I called Joe in Miami and he encouraged me to take the role. He said he would visit on weekends when he could get away.

We rehearsed in New York. There was a number called "Who's That Woman" that required everyone to tap dance like crazy. It had been a showstopper in the original production on Broadway. Steve Brookvar, our choreographer, had been Michael Bennett's assistant and wanted to duplicate that number. Vivian and I could dance but Selma, Lynn and Hildegarde really had a problem, so we rehearsed it over and over. It was difficult enough for them to just walk down the ramps to the music. It's not easy to learn tap in ten days.

We opened in Hyannis Port for a week and the show was a pretty big success. We were all on the bus ready to leave for our next town, except for Lynn Bari. By the time she came down, Steve Brookvar was livid. He delivered a big speech about the importance of everybody being on time with no exceptions. From the back of the bus, the throaty voice of Madame Bari spoke up. "Mr. Brookvar! I'll have you know I was ready on time but there was no one to take my f—— bag down to the f—— bus. Hereafter, if you have anything to say to me, *tap* it out!"

That seemed to set the tone for the tour. The next eight months were a laugh a minute.

During one performance, Hildegarde forgot the long gloves that had always been her trademark. It threw her so off-balance that she forgot the lyrics to her song, "Paree."

All the ladies requested small refrigerators in their rooms at the various hotels. They were nice to have for snacks after the show when everything else was closed. When we arrived at most of the hotels, we were all disappointed because only Selma's room had a refrigerator. She always called ahead and told them she was diabetic and needed a fridge for her insulin. Liar, liar, pants on fire!

Selma was a good comedy writer and later very funny on *Night Court*, but she wasn't funny to us.

At first, Joe visited only on the weekends, but as the tour extended, he decided to leave his job at the Racquet Club and come with me. He arrived in a brand new Mark IV and I can't tell you how happy I was to say goodbye to those wild bus rides. From then on, we rode to the theater in style.

Joe loved every minute of the tour and was very useful to everyone. He acted as a sort of road manager. At each stop, he'd locate the best restaurants and convince them to stay open for us after the show. No matter where we were, he always managed to find a tennis game. He didn't know any strangers.

The whole cast adored him. He always came up with the latest jokes and kept them laughing.

When the *Follies* tour ended, we returned to Florida, packed everything and moved to my home in California. It was an interesting drive with three cats and all of my feather boas.

After we got settled in, Joe became the managing director of a swinging place in Beverly Hills called Derricks. Richard Simmons was his Maitre d' and every star in Hollywood hung out there. Ed McMahon was there every night. The food was sensational and they added a piano bar off the lobby where George Burns, Johnnie Ray and others would get up and sing.

One night, Richard Simmons followed Barbra Streisand into the ladies room. When she asked what he was doing in there, he said, "I have just as much right to be here as you do!" But he left fast.

A woman by the name of Judy Thomas bought the place and her husband Derrick was the chef. Judy had great ideas and it was a hot place for about a year. Unfortunately, she overextended herself and had to give it up. She picked up so many checks that it certainly wasn't a total surprise. We were all sorry to see it go. It was such a fun place.

I was offered a part in *Mind with the Dirty Man* at the Union Plaza Hotel in Las Vegas. The play had been a big hit in Hollywood where Don Knotts had the starring role. Phil Ford was hired to play my husband and the part of a young porno queen was to be played by Marilyn Chambers of *Behind the Green Door* fame.

The first day of rehearsal, I looked for the blonde bombshell who was reportedly sex personified. When I finally met Miss Chambers, she was a young girl who was the picture of innocence. Marilyn had been hired to be the model on the cover of the Ivory Snow box, which pictured a mother holding a baby. When Proctor and Gamble discovered she was a porno queen, they quickly recalled all the Ivory Snow boxes.

Marilyn was a former gymnast who claimed she wasn't getting anywhere playing it straight so she called Chuck Traynor and asked him to manage her. She hoped he would do for her what he had done for Linda Lovelace when he was married to her. And did he ever. He married her and became her manager.

The demure-looking Miss Chambers thought nothing of opening the door naked when the bellman delivered something. Never had so much been seen by so many! There were a lot of happy bellmen at the Union Plaza that year.

Marilyn and I shared the same dresser. One night, our dresser asked if I'd seen the diamond ring Chuck had given to Marilyn. When I said no, she promptly asked Marilyn to come to my dressing room to show it to me. Marilyn walked in, lifted her leg and there was the diamond attached to her whatsit!

When I recovered myself, I asked her why she did it.

"Well, 'it' has done so much for me," she said. "I thought 'it' deserved a present."

Wow.

Sammy Davis Jr. was one of Marilyn's frequent backstage visitors. He bought her a stunning mink coat. I guess Sammy decided the upper part of her anatomy deserved a present also!

Maynard Sloate, the producer, asked me one night if I thought Joe would be interested in playing the part of the priest. The original actor, Bill Morey, was leaving the show and Joe bore a remarkable resemblance to him. I told him Joe wouldn't be interested and told Joe the story. "Can you imagine? Maynard thought you might be interested in playing the priest…ha, ha, ha!"

To my infinite surprise, Joe said he'd love to do it.

Joe made a great priest. He had fun with the role and only missed his entrance once or twice. He hated to interrupt his jokes to the Keno girls.

On Joe's opening night, he came out to take his bow and a whole row of his tennis buddies pummeled the stage with tennis balls.

Mind with the Dirty Man ran a year in Vegas, longer than any straight play in the history of the gambling city. I went with it to Sydney, Australia in 1975 where Keenan Wynn was my co-star. No porno queen played my daughter this time, just an Aussie Marilyn Monroe lookalike with a broad accent and a behind to match.

The show didn't repeat the success it had enjoyed in Las Vegas. The Australian Actors Equity would only allow two Americans in the cast and it didn't quite work with everyone else sounding like Crocodile Dundee. It was such an American play.

We spent three months there and went on to Japan and Manila where we stayed in Imelda Marcos' Hotel. I tried to see her shoe collection but she wouldn't let me. She did pick up the tab though.

Joe and I were away from home a lot then. We spent four months in New Orleans where I played Mama Rose in *Gypsy*. Storer Boone, the producer, offered Joe the part of Herbie but I told him to look for someone else. I didn't think he was qualified to play it. He couldn't carry a tune.

There were several smaller roles that were perfect for him. He played "Cigar" and "Mr. Gladstone" and several others. Each time he wore a different disguise. I never knew what to expect.

The stage manager found a dog to play "Chowsie," a cute mutt someone had deserted in her apartment building. She suggested we try him out. We named him Buster and from the first day, that dog had show business written all over him. In the song "Have an Egg Roll, Mr. Goldstone," there was a line "Have a coke, have a smoke." On the smoke line, Buster would take the cigar out of Joe's mouth and put it in his own. He did it every show and the audience went wild!

At the end of the run, I wanted to take Buster back to California but Joe wanted none of that. We were already traveling with three cats. I won out. Buster came anyway and we had him for fifteen years.

During Joe's previous marriage, he had gone to South Africa to make a movie over a period of a year's time. He was supposed to send for his wife but was having such a good time he never did. He came back a year later and she welcomed him with open arms.

In 1998, Joe was offered a job in Australia. He flew over there but the job didn't work out so I told him to come home. I had no desire to take that long trip to join him. He was gone for three months. He visited New

Zealand and had a marvelous time skiing and making new friends.

Joe forgot that he was married to a different girl this time.

I packed all his clothes and moved them out to the house in Malibu. When he came back, I had his son pick him up. Joe never had a shock like that in his life.

We reconciled some time later when he followed me back to New York.

Joe is a clown and he thinks like a single man. Life for him is a constant party. I've often told him that he married the wrong sister.

I made a movie at Walt Disney, a musical called *Pete's Dragon*. The cast included Helen Reddy, Red Buttons, Mickey Rooney, Jim Dale, Shelley Winters and Jim Backus. It was the first time I'd ever worked with my ex-brother-in-law.

The makeup man put some age on me and I played a mean schoolteacher. Every time I had to hit that cute little boy with a ruler, I'd apologize. When shooting for the day was over, I always made it a point to say goodnight to everyone in my regular makeup. I couldn't stand to let them think I always looked that bad. One of the cameramen was just too cute.

When the movie was finished, Joe and I spent some time in the little place we bought in Malibu at Paradise Cove. Joe had always lived near the water. He loved to swim in the ocean but seldom used our pool. He preferred to drive to the beach at Santa Monica with his pal, Dick Van Patten.

I considered Paradise Cove a perfect weekend getaway but Joe was spending more and more time out there. I do not share his enthusiasm for the beach. I loved it when I was young and could enjoy getting a suntan but now that's a no no. I prefer our city home in Toluca Lake so we compromise. He comes to town for parties, balls and Bar Mitzvahs and I spend most weekends out at the beach. Paradise Cove is a lively little community and it's party time always. No one locks his or her doors. It's the only safe place I know of in this crazy world.

Joe traveled with me when I appeared on several cruises. One was a Sitmar Cruise to Alaska. Mel Torme was on board to entertain, as were Rose Marie and her accompanist, Michael Feinstein, who was then unknown. Michael was seasick for nearly the entire trip but that didn't stop him from entertaining us after the show with his wonderful repertoire of old songs. Unusual for one so young.

Mel and I had opened the Thunderbird Hotel in Las Vegas, so we were old friends. One night after the first show, he came off so depressed because of an unenthusiastic audience.

In an effort to cheer him up, Joe said, "Don't worry, Mel. I'll see that you get a standing ovation the second show."

To which Mel replied, "That's impossible. The average age on this ship is deceased."

He did get a standing ovation, however, and he didn't need Joe's help.

Jane and Joe on their first date in Miami Beach when Joe had the Racquet Club there

Joe Hecht with sons, Lindsay and Joe, Jr.

With Jim Backus in Pete's Dragon

With Mel Torme on the Sitmar Cruise to Alaska

The Night The Laughter Died

In 1986, I was appearing in Atlanta with Mickey Rooney in *The Laugh's on Me*. I received a call from Deedee who was hysterical. She had just come from taking my sister to the doctor. He had informed Deedee that her mother had cancer and only had about six weeks to live.

I closed in Atlanta two days later and went directly back to Hollywood to see Betty. She had gone to read for a part at Disney. She was not aware of her condition because Deedee asked the doctor not to tell her how serious her illness was. I was with her every day for the next six weeks. Just like Helen, she kept up a front. Every day at five, the actors in the building would meet at her apartment for cocktails. Her sense of humor never stopped.

On her last day, a young doctor came in to help her and she called out in her hoarse voice, "He's cute. Ask him if he wants a drink." That night, exactly six weeks to the day, she left us. I was holding her hand and she suddenly looked up as if she saw something. Then, she closed her eyes.

Deedee and her husband, Stuart Wolpert, were writing and producing *The Facts of Life* at NBC. I called them at the studio to tell them the sad news.

With all our differences, we had great love for each other and the last few years we were closer than we had ever been.

Betty moved to California after Lew died. They had both been heavy smokers and both ended up dying of lung cancer. Toward the end of her life, Betty lost her voice almost entirely and was reduced to writing notes. I treasure those notes.

Deedee and I made funeral arrangements at Forest Lawn and held a memorial service at the Sportman's Lodge. Everyone who knew Betty loved her and said as much at the service.

When *Entertainment Tonight* called and asked for lifetime highlights and her age, I knocked off three years, whispering toward heaven, "That's the last favor I'm doing for you. From now on, you do your own negotiations."

I returned to Chicago to continue the show with Mickey and it helped a lot to get my mind off the unhappy events of the last six weeks. Mickey was very understanding. He had always liked Betty and shared my sadness.

The death of a sibling seems to drive home the importance of living life to the fullest while we are here. Betty certainly did that.

When I got home from Chicago, it truly hit home that Betty was no longer around. I missed just talking to her, hearing her rave about her two grandchildren and how proud she was of Deedee who was an accomplished writer. I never went back to Betty's apartment and told the superintendent to just invite the people in the building to take anything they wanted. Neither Deedee nor I wanted any reminders. Betty's role in our lives was sadly over. But, it was over. I hope wherever she and Helen are, they are having a drink together.

Betty

Life Goes On

Joe and I took a trip to Berlin when The Wall came down. The excitement of the German people on that New Year's Eve was a scene I'll never forget. Champagne bottles everywhere. People dancing on top of the wall. The first pass through the Brandenburg Gate. History in the making.

On the way home we stopped in London for a few weeks. as is our custom once a year. We saw some shows and visited with our friend, Jodie Wilson, and her fiancé, Des O'Conner. Des is the Englishman's Johnny Carson.

Sometime later, Joe and I went on a cruise to South America on the Crystal Harmony where I gave a series of lectures and showed videos of *The Honeymooners* and of Betty and me on Sullivan's show. Neither Joe nor I had been to that part of the world before and it was fabulous.

Back home for the holidays, I was on my way to Betty Aidman's Christmas party with my pal Irene Mariano. We stopped in a Christian Science Reading Room to buy a book and two young black men came in behind us and locked the door.

"Give me your money and your jewelry or I'll blow your brains out," one shouted, his gun focused on the poor saleswoman who was wearing a diamond pendant.

I was wearing two diamond rings that Walter had given me many birthdays ago. I fumbled with them both and finally stashed the larger of the two in my pocket. I was not about to give them up without a struggle.

The woman behind the counter was very "God Is Love." She said, "Oh, you don't want to do this. I don't believe that's even a real gun."

He said, "You want me to prove it to you, lady?" and cocked the gun.

The saleswoman was convinced. "On second thought, I believe you."

The whole time, Irene kept saying, "I don't believe it. I don't believe it."

To which I replied, "You'd better believe it and keep quiet."

He took my ring and watch but when he reached for my handbag, I just couldn't hand it over. All I could think of was how I would have to stand in line at the DMV for two hours in order to get a new license. When I kept asking for it, he looked at me like I was crazy.

I guess I was a little crazy because I had the ring in my pocket and a gun in my face. All I wanted was the damned license. He refused to give it to me but we were alive and we didn't have to drop to the floor and be tied up like they do in the movies.

They left as quickly as they came, only a little richer. And I was facing a whole afternoon at the Department of Motor Vehicles.

A Christmas Farewell

Every Christmas, Joe and I have a big party for all our friends. One Christmas, I'd heard Gleason was in town shooting the sequel to *Smokey and the Bandit* with Mac Davis. Jackie and Marilyn were staying at the Beverly Hills Hotel and I invited them to my annual Christmas party. I wasn't sure they'd show up because Jackie wasn't that much of a partygoer.

After all the other guests had arrived, The Great One appeared at the door. He had had a little surgery done and looked slightly different. When I introduced him, people thought I'd hired a Jackie Gleason lookalike.

I had a tough time convincing them he was the real McCoy. Marilyn said he'd been ready since five o'clock. The party started at 6:30. He spent the waiting time in the Polo Lounge but he was sober when he arrived.

I was later informed of his death at a dinner party at my home. Some insensitive reporter called and asked me how I felt about his death and if I could recall any funny stories about him. That was the first I had heard. It was such a shock. I was in tears the rest of the night. I truly loved the man.

To the moon, Jackie.

Rehearsing with Art

The Honeymooners

Jane and Joe's annual Christmas party, 1990

The Honeymooners

After Words

Writing this book has given me a chance to look back at my life and I've come to the conclusion it has been pretty good. I've had my share of disappointments, but on a scale of one to ten, it was about a nine.

I may have never gotten into show business if my mother hadn't pushed me onto the stage of the Bushnell Memorial. I don't know if I've lived up to my mother's expectations but I've never drank or smoked, and two out of three is pretty good.

I still enjoy working although I have admittedly dropped my subscriptions to *Variety* and *The Hollywood Reporter*. The things that really matter now are my home, my friends, and my family. Joe has three grown sons, Lindsay, Randy and Joe Jr. The latter is the only one who's married and lives in California. He and his lovely wife, Sandy, produced a son who weighed only a pound and a half when he was born. I'm happy to say, he's twelve years old today and is as healthy and strong as any kid on the block.

I am still very close to Betty's daughter, Deedee. She and Stuart have two great offspring. Baley, a dead ringer for Gwyneth Paltrow, wants to be an actress. Ben, 20, longs to be a writer like his father. Stuart recently formed a rock and roll band called The Mid-Life Crisis. The group is comprised of fellow writers who play and sing as well as any band I've seen. I should know. I recently boogied to their music until midnight.

Volunteer work for the Actor's Home and recording for the blind are two favorite projects and there is still time for appearances on the cruise ships and at the autograph and collectors' shows. Although I lead a busy life, I still take time to smell the roses.

Life goes on and on!

What'd ya know? I received a call from Riff Markowitz, the producer and creator of the most successful stage show in Palm Springs. The fabulous *Palm Springs Follies* is in its twelfth year and is sold out at every performance. No one in the cast is under sixty and they are all just gorgeous and talented and can kick and tap like the pros they used to be. I was asked to join the cast as the special guest star for a six-week run. Could I refuse? I don't think so!

So, I dusted off the old arrangements, bought some jazzy clothes, got out the Jaguar, grabbed my dog Angel, and Joe and I were off to Palm Springs for another showbiz adventure. What a ball it was to stand on stage again to a packed house and sing my little heart out.

JANE KEAN

Publicity photo

Credits

Theater

1940   *Hi Ya Gentlemen*
1943   *Early to Bed*
1945   *Are You With It?*
1945   *The Girl from Nantucket*
1947   *Call Me Mister*
1949   *Along Fifth Avenue*
1951   *Born Yesterday*
1955   *Ankles Aweigh*
1958   *Anything Goes*
1959   *Say, Darling*
1960   *Hit the Deck*
1960   *Sketch Book* (Las Vegas)
1961   *Will Success Spoil Rock Hunter?*
1961   *Happy Hunting*
1961   *Pajama Game*
1961   *Show Boat*
1961   *Goodbye Charlie*
1962   *Guys and Dolls*
1962   *Gentlemen Prefer Blondes*
1962-63 *Carnival*
1963   *Brigadoon*
1964   *Kiss Me, Kate*
1967   *Luv*
1970   *Gypsy*
1971   *Light Up the Sky*
1973   *Follies*
1974   *Dames at Sea*

1974	*Mind with the Dirty Man* (Las Vegas)
1975	*Mind with the Dirty Man* (Australia)
1977	*Last of the Red Hot Lovers*
1979	*Barefoot in the Park*
1980	*Gypsy*
1981	*Threads*
1985	*Sabrina Fair*
1986	*The Laughs on Me*
1988	*Steel Magnolias*
1988	*The Women*
1989	*The Music Man*
1990	*On Golden Pond*
1990	*Light Up the Sky*
1990	*Deathtrap*
1990	*Arthur*
1994	*Mind with the Dirty Man* (with Mickey Rooney)
1995	*On Golden Pond*
2000	*Fiddler on the Roof*
2003	*Palm Springs Follies*

Films

1941	*Sailors on Leave*
1942	*Flying with Music*
1977	*Pete's Dragon*
1977	*Chatterbox*
1984	*Madman of the People*
1985	*Explorers* (voice)
1999	*Gideon*

Television

Regular

1965-66	*Day of Our Lives*
1966-70	*The Jackie Gleason Show*
1989-90	*Paradise*

Guest Shots

1948	*The RCA Thanksgiving Show*
1949	*Fireside Theatre* ("Meet My Sister")
1950	*Toast of the Town*
1950	*Ford Star Revue*
1950	*Cavalcade of Stars*
1951	*The Frank Sinatra Show*
1951	*Showtime USA*
1951	*All-Star Revue*
1951	*Faye Emerson's Wonderful Town*
1951	*Arthur Murray Party*
1952	*All-Star Summer Revue*
1953	*Texaco Star Theatre*
1953	*Season's Greetings*
1954	*Toast of the Town*
1955	*Shower of Stars* ("Show Stoppers")
1955	*Strike It Rich*
1955	*Toast of the Town*
1956	*This Is Show Business*
1956	*The Amazing Dunninger*
1958	*Club Oasis*
1959	*The Phil Silvers Show* ("Doberman, Missing Heir")
1959	*The Phil Silvers Show* ("The Bilko Boycott")
1960	*Be Our Guest*
1962	*Follow the Sun* ("Not Aunt Charlotte")
1962	*The New Loretta Young Show* ("Decision at Midnight")
1962	*Mr. Magoo's Christmas Carol*
1964	*The Danny Thomas Show*
1966	*The Lucy Show*
1967	*The Merv Griffin Show*
1968	*The Joey Bishop Show*
1970	*Love, American Style* ("Love and the Millionaires")
1974	*Cannon* ("A Killing in the Family")
1976	*The Honeymooners - The Second Honeymoon*
1977	*The Honeymooners Christmas*

1978	*The Honeymooners Valentine Special*
1978	*The Honeymooners Christmas Special*
1981	*Making a Living*
1982	*King's Crossing*
1985	*Scarecrow and Mrs. King* ("A Little Sex, a Little Scandal")
1985	*The Facts of Life* ("Men for All Seasons")
1986	*Morningstar/Eveningstar*
1989	*Growing Pains* ("Mom of the Year")
1991	*Dream On* ("Toby or Not Toby")
1994	*Madman of the People* ("What a Mouth You Have, Grammy")

Walter Tetley
FOR CORN'S SAKE
by Ben Ohmart
and Charles Stumpf

ISBN: 1-59393-000-3

$24.95

WALTER TETLEY (1915-1975) was the quintessential kid voice of radio. His distinguished voice career began in the early 1930s and lasted until radio's final years in the 1950s. He was also a very private person who never gave interviews, instead choosing to immerse himself in charity and voice work throughout most of his life.

For the FIRST time in print—finally a complete biography on one of radio's most beloved character actors. Including many **RARE PHOTOS** and **THOU-SANDS OF CREDITS**, most of which have never been seen or discussed in any article or book. That is because **this biography has been written with the aid of Walter's personal scrapbooks!**

From The Great Gildersleeve to Peabody and Sherman—and beyond.

Including a detailed account of Walter's 1930s public appearances.

FOR FANS OF OLD TIME RADIO—THIS IS THE BOOK TO SAVOR!

___ YES, please send me ___ copies of *Walter Tetley* for just $24.95 each.

___ YES, I would like more information about your other publications.

Add $2 postage per book. For non-US orders, please add $4 per book for airmail, in US funds. Payment must accompany all orders. Or buy online with Paypal at bearmanormedia.com.

My check or money order for $_____ is enclosed. Thank you.

NAME _____

ADDRESS _____

CITY/STATE/ZIP_____

EMAIL _____

Checks payable to: BearManor Media * P O Box 750 * Boalsburg, PA 16827
info@ritzbros.com

HOLLYWOOD'S GOLDEN AGE

As Told By One Who Lived It All

Edward Dmytryk

ISBN: 0-9714570-4-2 $17.95

A legend remembers the good old days of films...

Edward Dmytryk, director of *The Caine Mutiny, Murder, My Sweet, Hitler's Children* and a host of other classic movies, has written a powerful memoir of his early days in Hollywood. From peeking in at the special effects for *The Ten Commandmants*, the original silent film, to his first job as an editor, slowly, patiently splicing film...Dmytryk's brilliantly written and **until now unpublished** look back on old Hollywood is a joy you won't be able to put down.

FOR FANS OF OLD HOLLYWOOD—THIS IS THE BOOK TO SAVOR!